THE
HEALING
JOURNEY
THROUGH GRIEF

Your Journal for
Reflection and Recovery

Phil Rich, EdD, MSW

John Wiley & Sons, Inc.

NEW YORK ✦ CHICHESTER ✦ WEINHEIM ✦ BRISBANE ✦ SINGAPORE ✦ TORONTO

Library of Congress Cataloging-in-Publication Data:
Rich, Phil.
    The healing journey through grief: your journal for reflection and recovery / by Phil Rich.
        p.   cm.
        ISBN 0-471-29565-5 (pbk. : alk. paper)
        1. Grief.   2. Bereavement—Psychological aspects.   3. Death—Psychological aspects.   4. Loss (Psychology)   5.   Diaries—Therapeutic use.   6. Psychotherapy—Problems, exercises, etc.   I. Title.
        BF575.G7R53 1999
        155.9'37—dc21

98-22978

CIP

Printed in the United States of America.

10 9 8 7 6 5 4 3 2

Contents

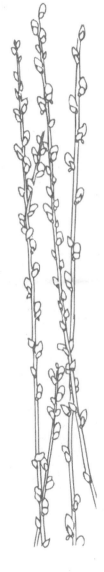

About *The Healing Journey Through Grief*

SOMEONE IMPORTANT IN your life has died, and with their passing your life has changed. How do you cope with the powerful emotions, chaos, and confusion that follow such a loss? What do you do to ease the pain and grief you feel? How can you carry on and eventually return to your normal daily routine?

The Healing Journey Through Grief is a guided personal journal, intended to help you work through your loss. It will provide you with information about grief and the grieving process. And it will give you a means of working through your grief: a place to write down your reflections and exercises to help you make sense of your loss and find ways to rebuild your life.

This journal/workbook is primarily for those experiencing grief resulting from the death of someone meaningful in their lives. However, *The Healing Journey Through Grief* can help with grief, no matter what its source. There are many causes of grief and many forms of loss—the loss of a job, the loss of a relationship, the loss of something important, perhaps even vital, in your life and to your well-being. You may feel deep grief caused by injury to family members, to friends, or even to yourself. There is

"Nothing that grieves us can be called little: by the eternal laws of proportion a child's loss of a doll and a king's loss of a crown are events of the same size."
—MARK TWAIN

v

no source of grief that should be considered too small or inconsequential to examine.

Whatever the source of your grief, it is important that you work through it. *The Healing Journey Through Grief* can help you do this. This unique journal can be a consoling companion and a valuable guidebook on your journey, as you come to terms with your loss and the rebuilding of your life.

I

Embarking on
Your Journey

Grief Work

IF YOU'RE IN the active process of mourning the death of a loved family member or friend, *The Healing Journey Through Grief* is for you. For some, grief is a relatively quick journey, lasting a few months. For others, it may take years to resolve grief and recover from a loss—mourning has no time limit. You may be in the earliest stages of the mourning process, or you may be far into your grief. Wherever you are in your bereavement, *The Healing Journey Through Grief* can help you come to terms with your loss.

The process of working through grief—dealing with the emotions and the situations caused by a death as well as the impact of the loss on mind, body, and spirit—is frequently referred to as grief work. *The Healing Journey Through Grief* can aid you in your grief work by helping you explore your loss, identify and understand your feelings about it, and figure out ways to rebuild your life. This personal journal can be a comforting and illuminating companion in your grief work. Writing in a journal gives you a

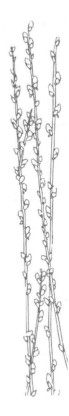

way to collect your thoughts, provides you with a tool to reflect on and interpret your feelings, and gives you a place to record your thoughts and memories.

Sharing Your Grief and Getting Help

Writing in a journal gives you a way to collect your thoughts, provides you with a tool to reflect on and interpret your feelings, and gives you a place to record your thoughts and memories.

The very nature of grief work is difficult, and the act of writing about and exploring your painful feelings may be uncomfortable. Some entries in *The Healing Journey Through Grief* may evoke difficult and painful feelings, which may make you feel vulnerable. Seek help whenever you find yourself feeling especially pained, fragile, or lost. A support network—family, friends, neighbors, members of your church or temple, or others in your community —is essential during your grief work, but even so this might not be enough. If you find the grief process especially difficult to bear, seek help from a trained grief counselor, therapist, clergy member, or social worker or through a grief support group. In fact, it's quite possible that you've discovered this book through such a connection.

Moving Through *The Healing Journey Through Grief*

If you're working with a counselor, she or he may assign a specific chapter or journal entry for you. If you're working on your own, where should you start? *The Healing Journey Through Grief* was designed to be used in the sequence presented, and the progression of chapters and journal entries coincides with the stages most typical in the grieving process. Although you may want to glance ahead, don't rush through this book. Just as you can't recover from grief overnight, you shouldn't try to complete your journal in a day or two. There is no "right" pace for grieving, but you may wish to read through one chapter a week and complete the journal entries within that chapter. This will give you time to reread and think about what you've written, before moving on to the next phase of your grief work.

Although it's recommended that you work through *The Healing Journey Through Grief* in the order presented, this may not always be possible or desirable. You may come to an entry that you aren't ready for. If so, skip it, and come back to that entry at a later point in your grief work. You may also want to move in a different sequence because of an immediate need to deal with pressing emotional or life issues. Each chapter and journal entry in this book can stand on its own, and you can pick the order best suited to your needs. The next chapter, "A Road Map to Grief," will help you assess where you are in your grief work and help you pick the best place to start your healing journey.

Making Yourself Comfortable

Regardless of the chapter or entry you start with, you need to decide which conditions and environment will best support your journal writing. Here are some suggestions that may make the process more comfortable for you.

- Try to set a regular schedule for working through your journal, preferably at a time of day when you're fresh and have the most energy.
- Take breaks during your writing if you need to. Stretching your legs can also give your mind a break.
- Consider playing some quiet music or other relaxing sounds in the background.
- Make sure you have pens, pencils, coloring pens, or other writing and drawing instruments that are comfortable for you to use as you write. Pick a place to read and write that will be physically comfortable for you.
- Pick a place to read and write that will be emotionally com-

fortable for you. It might be a quiet and private area, or it might be a community and public arena.

- If writing is emotionally difficult for you, or you find your feelings or thoughts overwhelming at times, consider having a comforting picture or object nearby or something else that might be familiar and safe.

- Make sure there's someone available for you to talk to after you write if you think you may need some personal contact or support.

- Once you've completed an entry, reread what you've written. Reflecting on what you've written can help you gain new insights.

Make sure there's someone available for you to talk to after you write if you think you may need some personal contact or support.

Using the Entries

The styles for different journal entries in *The Healing Journey Through Grief* vary and are often different from one another, and each entry is provided only once. There are some entry formats that you may especially like using, and there are entries that you'll want to repeat more than once. Feel free to keep a supplemental journal in addition to this book, where you can add your "spillover" thoughts or write additional entries. You may also want to photocopy certain blank entries in order to complete that entry more than once.

The Value of Your Grief Journal

Your journal can be of great value as you work through your bereavement, and it can help you understand and build order out of the emotional turmoil that has followed your loss. But its importance is built directly upon your use of it: if you use your grief journal on a regular basis, it will be an important tool in your grief work.

2

A Road Map to Grief

"No one ever told me that grief felt so like fear."
—C. S. LEWIS

BOB

Since my wife died unexpectedly seven months ago, I've been shattered emotionally, and my life is in constant turmoil. At times, I'm not sure if I'm coming or going. I've had family members pass away before, and once lost a friend to a heart attack, but those deaths didn't affect me the way that Terri's has. Nothing can prepare you for that kind of loss.

Some days are better than others. Although I'm putting one foot in front of the other, I have no spirit or energy. I can't picture my future, and I'm filled with memories of the past. And overwhelming emotions still poke through unexpectedly. One moment, I feel very angry because I've lost Terri—at her and at the world for taking her away. At other times, I'm just too sad to move or even cry.

The worst part is, I don't know if I'll ever feel better. And part of me doesn't want to, because that might mean Terri wasn't really important. Sometimes, I can't quite picture her face, and that frightens me. Does this mean she'll just fade away? And if I don't remember her, who will? In some ways, the more time that passes, the more confused I am. I don't know what to feel or do anymore, or how I'm supposed to feel.

GRIEF IS AN inevitable part of life. And, as you've picked up this book, you're probably in the midst of trying to cope with the loss of someone you love. Philosophical musings about life and death probably don't help much, and you may be finding that the support and comfort offered by family and friends isn't helping you work through the pain you're feeling.

So what can help? First, developing an understanding of the grief process that most people in your situation experience can be helpful. Even though every loss is unique, and each person irreplaceable, there are some common phases to the mourning process. If you understand these "stages" of grief, you'll see that you aren't alone in your confusion, turmoil, and pain—and that things improve as you progress through the stages.

The second thing that can help is tuning in to how you're feeling and what you're experiencing, and then expressing those emotions and thoughts. Most societies have mourning rituals (like sitting shivah or holding wakes), so you probably had a support network to lean on right after your loss. But as time passes, friends and family get back to their own lives, and it can become hard to find someone with whom to share your feelings.

Even if you have an ongoing support network, many people don't know what to say to someone in the throes of grief, so they fall back on platitudes like "time will heal," or "you've got to move on." Although they're only trying to help, these kinds of messages can really hurt because they imply that there's a set norm for how long and in what ways you can mourn. The passage of time can help, but the bottom line is that if you are not ready to "move on," no amount of prodding or pushing can help.

You can, however, help yourself as you progress through the stages of grief by identifying and working through your feelings

Even though every loss is unique, and each person irreplaceable, there are some common phases to the mourning process.

and experiences. The journal entries throughout this book are designed to help you with that process. You can use these entries to sort through your emotions, record your thoughts, and reflect on your experiences. And the process of writing about your past with your lost loved one, your present state of mind and, eventually, the future you envision can help you move forward and heal. The first step toward that healing is understanding where you are *now*.

The Grief Continuum

Although your grief experience is intensely personal, there are some fairly typical stages of bereavement. These range from initial shock to anguish and despair, once the realization of the loss sinks in, to eventual acceptance. Within each stage are specific emotional and psychological tasks, which must be worked through completely before you can move on to successfully complete the tasks of the next stage.

Although these stages are generally a predictable part of the mourning process, grief doesn't always move in a straight line. The stages tend to flow together and fluctuate, so it's not always possible to tell which stage you are in. Emotions seesaw, and overwhelming feelings pass and then return. Moods wash in and out like the tide. Just when you think you are "over" it, a sound, smell, or image can send you back into emotional turmoil. This back-and-forth movement may occur over a period of months or even years.

Although they may vary from person to person, it's not unusual for the active stages of grieving to last one to two full years or more. *The Healing Journey Through Grief* can help you track the stages and their fluctuations and enable you to reflect on them throughout the entire period of mourning. It can also assist you in doing the necessary grief work, which includes:

- facing the reality of your loss
- working through painful memories
- experiencing the full range of emotions associated with loss
- coping with the situational and lifestyle changes resulting from your loss
- adapting to the loss and reconfiguring your life

Stages of Grief

The goals of grief work are not to find ways to avoid or bypass the emotional turmoil and upsets brought by your loss. Instead, they involve working through the tasks and emotions of each stage of grief.

The goals of grief work are not to find ways to avoid or bypass the emotional turmoil and upsets brought by your loss. Instead, they involve working through the tasks and emotions of each stage of grief. Grief work can be broken down into three stages: acclimation and adjustment, emotional immersion and deconstruction, and reclamation and reconciliation.

STAGE 1: ACCLIMATION AND ADJUSTMENT

Stage 1 is a period of acclimation and adjustment, in which the primary issues faced by the newly bereaved can be broken down into four tasks.

1. *Adjusting.* You come to accept that your loved one is gone, and you begin making sense of the new set of circumstances in your life.

2. *Functioning.* It's a cruel irony that the practicalities of mortgage payments, funeral experiences, insurance claims, hospital bills, disbursing of possessions, or getting back to work hit you at a time when you are least up to facing these issues. But despite your loss, you need to accept that you still have a life to lead and must continue to deal with your everyday responsibilities.

3. *Keeping in check.* The temptation in the face of a tremendous loss is to emotionally shut down or, at the other ex-

treme, to let your emotions and behaviors flow unchecked. One of the tasks of Stage 1 is to find a way to manage your thoughts, feelings, and behaviors.

4. *Accepting support.* Often, you don't have to face your loss alone. Learning to accept the kindness, help, encouragement, and support of the friends, family, and others who populate your life is important.

STAGE 2: EMOTIONAL IMMERSION AND DECONSTRUCTION

Stage 2 is one of emotional immersion and deconstruction, and it incorporates the most active aspects of grief work. It's not that this stage is any more intense than the first stage—in fact, it's difficult to imagine that anything could be more intense than the period immediately following a loss—but during Stage 2, you're likely to become deeply immersed in your feelings, and very internally focused. It's also quite common to undergo a "deconstruction" of your values and beliefs, as you question why your loved one was taken from you. Four tasks associate with Stage 2 are:

1. *Contending with reality.* Once the shock of the death has passed, you must begin to more fully resume your normal life, accept that your loved one is gone, and deal with the life changes resulting from your loss.

2. *Development of insight.* Stage 2 is a time for soul-searching: the exploration of your place in the world, your current emotional state, and the meaning of your thoughts and feelings.

3. *Reconstructing personal values and beliefs.* In the aftermath of the death and the many changes it may have brought, you need to find meaning in the world and establish what is, and isn't, important in your life.

4. *Acceptance and letting go.* Here the task is to fully accept the death and your feelings about it, find a way to let go of that which has passed, and begin to move toward that which will be.

STAGE 3: RECLAMATION AND RECONCILIATION

Stage 3 is a time for reclamation and reconciliation and is generally thought to be one marked by your "recovery" from grief. But the loss of someone close to you leaves a permanent mark on your life, in the sense that things can't be restored to the way they were before the death. However, you can begin to rebuild, creating a new life for yourself and reengaging with the world around you. As this stage ends, you'll become reconciled to the death itself and the changes it's brought to your life. Perhaps most important, you'll begin to live in the present, rather than the past, reestablish who you are in the world, and plan a future. The four primary tasks of this stage follow.

1. *Development of social relations.* Whereas Stage 2 was internally focused, Stage 3 is externally focused as you reestablish friendships and renew community connections.

2. *Decisions about changes in lifestyle.* Here you make long-term practical choices about how to proceed with your life, including where to live, how to spend your time, what to keep from your "old" life, and what to change.

3. *Renewal of self-awareness.* This task involves consolidating the things you've learned about yourself and your life through your grief work and building your daily life around this new self-awareness.

4. *Acceptance of responsibility.* The task here is to both maintain your support network and become increasingly self-reliant, taking responsibility for your own happiness, well-being, and life course.

CHECKPOINT: STAGES

Circle the letter that most closely describes where you are *right now* with each task.

Stage 1 Tasks	I'm not ready to deal with this task.	I'm working on this task.	I've completed this task.
Adjusting	A	B	C
Functioning	A	B	C
Keeping in check	A	B	C
Accepting support	A	B	C
Stage 2 Tasks			
Contending with reality	A	B	C
Development of insight	A	B	C
Reconstructing personal values and beliefs	A	B	C
Acceptance and letting go	A	B	C
Stage 3 Tasks			
Development of social relations	A	B	C
Decisions about changes in lifestyle	A	B	C
Renewal of self-awareness	A	B	C
Acceptance of responsibility	A	B	C

You'll return to this checkpoint periodically as you work through your healing journey.

GETTING LOCATED

You're now aware of the stages of grief and how they typically progress, and your Checkpoint entry has helped you identify where you are with respect to each of the grief work tasks. Look at the Checkpoint answers you've circled.

1. Which four tasks are the most relevant to you *now*, in your current grief stage?

a. _____

b. _____

c. _____

d. _____

2. What do the tasks you picked tell you about your current grief work?

_____

_____

_____

3. What's your current grief stage? (If it's difficult for you to easily identify your current grief stage, go directly to the next step in this entry.)

_____

4. Was it difficult for you to easily identify your current grief stage? If so, why?

_____

_____

_____

THINGS TO THINK ABOUT

- Does the idea that there are "stages" to grief fit your own bereavement experience?
- Are you feeling encouraged by what you've read so far, or does your grief journey seem overwhelming?

Feeling Your Grief

You now have a sense of your current grief stage. But identifying your location along this continuum may be emotionally difficult, especially if you have only just begun your grief work. You may find yourself feeling overwhelmed, dismayed, or discouraged by the tasks ahead. Remember to stop and get support or help if you're finding the process especially difficult, or just take a break if you need to.

How do you move from Stage 1 to Stage 3? *Wanting* to complete the tasks associated with each stage so that you can move on isn't enough. Grief work isn't a matter of willpower or tenacity — it's a matter of the heart. Although thinking about and reflecting on your loss is an important component of grief work, the key to healing is to allow yourself to *experience* the mass of feelings that have hit you since your loss and then sort through and express them.

Many people can identify a small group of emotions that they often experience. These emotions may have grown familiar and comfortable, even if they're unpleasant feelings, such as anger or sadness. People are quick to revert to familiar emotions, but they may not notice the web of other emotions that are often layered beneath and contributing to them. In fact, it's easy to get "stuck" in one emotional state. But to understand and manage intense emotions, you need to recognize, experience, and express *each* feeling. As you work through them, the intensity of each feeling will eventually fade to the point where you can function and move on.

To understand and manage intense emotions, you need to recognize, experience, and express each feeling.

What are you feeling *right now*? Are you confused by your feelings? Is it hard to pinpoint them? The next journal entry lists the emotions most commonly associated with grief. This checklist can help you sort out your feelings and select the appropriate chapter in *The Healing Journey Through Grief* to turn to to try to process your most intense emotions at the moment.

IDENTIFYING YOUR FEELINGS

Check all of the emotions that best describe what you are generally experiencing at this point in your bereavement.

___anger   Anger often feels like a physical thing. Your muscles   (7, 8, 13)
            tense up, and you may feel like yelling at someone or
            hitting something. Your rage may be aimed at yourself
            or your lost loved one, or you may find yourself getting
            angry at other people, society, or your spiritual beliefs.

___anxiety Anxiety is distinct from fear, and is often a generalized   (3, 7)
            feeling. If you're afraid, at least you know what scares
            you. If you're anxious, on the other hand, you're likely

to feel agitated without knowing exactly why. You
may experience cold sweats, hyperactivity, or edginess.

__bitterness   Life may feel very unjust, and you may feel cheated   (7, 8, 13)
and disappointed. You may feel jealous and resentful
toward others who still have what has been taken
from you, and you may feel victimized by fate.

__confusion   You may be unsure of what you're feeling, or your   (2–4)
feelings may change quickly. Your thoughts may be
unfocused, making it difficult for you to concentrate,
or you may have a hard time knowing what to do
and how best to make decisions.

__depression   Depression can be a general melancholic mood or a   (6–8)
full-blown experience that is all-encompassing and
seems to have no end. In a major depression your mood,
appetite, sleep, memory, and ability to concentrate are
seriously impaired. You may feel the impulse to do self-
destructive things in an effort to find relief.

__despair   Here you feel a sense of futility. It seems like things will   (7–9)
never get better, and the distress caused by death may
feel unbearable. Although you want to, you may not be
able to get your feelings out by crying, or you may be
unable to stop crying.

__detachment   You feel disconnected from the death, and detached   (5, 6, 15)
from life in general. The experience seems unreal, as
if it were happening to someone else. You simply pass
through life each day, your actions detached from your
thoughts and feelings.

__fear   You're scared of what life will be like now. You may be   (5–7)
fearful about your ability to cope emotionally, or you
may be uncertain about practical concerns like money,

raising the children, or where you'll live. You may
just be afraid, without really knowing why.

__feeling lost   Everything that you used to believe in is gone. You   (9, 14)
                      aren't sure where you fit in the world or who you are.
                      If religious or spiritual, your faith is shaken. If not, you
                      feel it unwise to ever have faith in a world where
                      nothing seems permanent.

__feeling   You simply can't cope with the barrage of emotions,   (3–5, 7–8)
overwhelmed   thoughts, and changes facing you. You feel like
                     running away, or escaping by using alcohol or drugs.
                     You want someone to come rescue you and make it
                     all go away.

__guilt   You may feel that you could have done more to help   (12–13)
                     or prevent the death. You may feel intense regret
                     about the way you behaved toward your loved one or
                     about promises you never kept. You may also feel guilty
                     about negative feelings you harbor toward your loved
                     one or mixed feelings about the death itself. It is also
                     common for the bereaved to feel guilty when they begin
                     to laugh and find pleasure in life once again or begin
                     new relationships. Or you may experience survivor
                     guilt—a sense of remorse that *you* remain alive while
                     your loved one has died.

__helplessness   Things seem out of control. You may think that if you   (5, 6, 9)
                     were powerless to prevent the death, then you can't
                     handle anything. You can't cope with the practicalities
                     of everyday life, and you feel unable to control or
                     manage your feelings.

__hopelessness   Life has no meaning. It seems there is no point to   (5, 6, 13)
                     anything, and things will never get better. Your feelings

and the tasks you face seem insurmountable, and you feel unable to ever overcome your loss.

__loneliness   There is no one who can understand your pain. There (5, 6, 11, 15) seems to be no one with whom to share things or from whom to seek comfort. These feelings may make you feel like withdrawing even further from those around you or the world at large.

__numbness   You are shut down emotionally. You feel nothing. (7, 8, 14) Everything is flat. Although you might be able to function and get through each day, it sometimes seems as if you are sleepwalking through life, unable to feel your emotions.

__preoccupation   You can't stop thinking about your loss. Perhaps (10–12) you keep replaying certain scenes over and over in your mind or agonize about who you might lose next. You can't concentrate on your everyday responsibilities or engage in a conversation without your mind wandering. Intrusive memories keep surfacing no matter what you do.

__sadness   Sorrow and heartbreak colors everything. You feel (7, 8, 14) your loss deeply, and it affects and pervades all you do. It is a mood that simply won't go away.

__shame   You may feel that you should be getting "over" your (3, 4, 7) feelings, or you may be ashamed to show them in front of family, friends, and others. You may also harbor feelings about the death or the fact that you are still alive that feel shameful to you and are difficult to share with others.

__shock   You are bewildered and confused. Even if prepared for (3, 4) the death, the situation doesn't seem real. The finality

of the situation leaves you feeling stunned, and you
may not be able to accept that your loved one is gone.
You keep hoping to wake up from a bad dream.

__vulnerability   Your faith in your own invulnerability is shattered. You   (9, 14)
                   are constantly aware of your own mortality and the
                   mortality of other important people in your life. You
                   feel exposed, without protection, to whatever destiny
                   or life hands you.

__yearning   You long for the deceased. It hurts so much that you   (10–15)
                   feel a constant pit in your stomach. You are constantly
                   aware of the absence of your loved one, and you feel
                   empty. Nothing can fill the void.

Of the feelings you checked off, which three are the most intense right now?

1. _____

2. _____

3. _____

If you want to work on any one of these feelings right away, turn to the chapters
whose numbers are given in parentheses to the right of each feeling on the list above.
If you decide to work through *The Healing Journey Through Grief* sequentially, you may
still want to come back to this list every now and then to see which feelings are most
pressing at any given time.

All this background information is intended to help you place
your grief in context so that you'll understand you're not alone
in your travels through the despair that follows the death of
someone close. Armed with that knowledge, it's now time for
you to begin your journey through the grief process. There are
likely to be bumps along the road and obstacles in your way, but
if you use this journal you'll not only have a travel guide but also a
companion on the road to healing the wound of loss.

CHECKING IN WITH YOURSELF

Complete these five sentences.

1. *As I complete this chapter, I feel like* . . . _____

_____

_____

2. *Right now, I'd like to* . . . _____

_____

_____

3. *Lately, I've been feeling like* . . . _____

_____

_____

4. *My most important current task is* . . . _____

_____

_____

5. *I feel like I most need to work on* . . . _____

_____

_____

THINGS TO THINK ABOUT

- Are there specific questions you need to answer for yourself before continuing with *The Healing Journey Through Grief*?
- Do you have a clear sense of the sorts of issues, feelings, and tasks that you'll be facing in your grief work?
- Will you work your way through *The Healing Journey Through Grief* in the sequence provided, or will you move through the book in your own order?
- Are the problems you're experiencing so severe or debilitating that you need support and help from a friend or assistance from a professional counselor?

3

Destination:

ADJUSTMENT

This is the Hour of
    Lead —
Remembered, if outlived,
As Freezing persons,
    recollect the Snow —
First Chill, then Stupor
    —then the letting go.
—**EMILY DICKINSON**

MICHELLE

I divorced several years ago. My marriage was never a successful one, and we had decided against having children. I did miss my ex-husband after the divorce, but I lived near my parents and we were always very close. They were a source or great comfort and importance in my life at that time.

In fact, we became even closer after my separation, and I rarely missed spending Saturday with them both. As they grew older, they came to depend on me more, and they became an even more important part of my life. My mother died last year, and my father passed away within eight months of her death.

It's been very difficult for me to adjust to their deaths. I lead a busy life, and have a wonderful job and close friends, but my parents filled a special and important need in my world. I find my evenings empty without them, and I still get sad as the weekend approaches, knowing I won't be spending Saturday with them, shopping with my mother and preparing their evening meal. I still find myself reaching for the phone when there's something on TV my father would enjoy or when I have news to share with my mom.

Although my life's moved on, I haven't been able to adjust to their absence or fill the hole their death has left in my life. I never imagined that at my age I would feel like an orphan—but I do.

FOR MANY, THE death of someone close comes out of the blue— the result of an accident or sudden trauma. Of course, some deaths can be anticipated, as in the case of an elderly parent or spouse or if there has been a terminal illness. But this doesn't make the situation any more bearable for the bereaved, or the loss any less devastating. Even if you're able to anticipate the loss of your loved one, death is something for which we are never truly prepared.

The goal of grief work is not to avoid the emotional aftermath of death but rather first to accept, then overcome, its impact on your life.

The goal of grief work is not to avoid the emotional aftermath of death but rather first to accept, then overcome, its impact on your life. And it's not the words of support or comfort offered by supporters, nor their advice, that makes the pain any less bearable—four hundred years ago, William Shakespeare observed that "every one can master a grief but he that has it."

It is your ability and willingness to honestly engage in grief work—to face and work through the tasks that follow loss— that will most help you get through this terribly difficult time in your life.

In Chapter 2, you read about the stages of grief that people most typically pass through as they work through their loss. But bear in mind that specific grief responses are as unique as each individual. Your grief experience can't be easily compared with the grief experienced by anyone else. You can't "judge" your grief, except by its effects on your ability to function in life *while* you grieve.

Your grief experience can't be easily compared with the grief experienced by anyone else. You can't "judge" your grief, except by its effects on your ability to function in life while you grieve.

You should be aware that the sometimes extreme emotions described in the previous chapter are "normal" experiences of grief. And the feelings, thoughts, and behaviors that follow a loss are expected. Everyone understands that you won't be able to attend work in the days following the death of someone close. Friends and colleagues expect you to cancel appointments and postpone the usual social conventions. In fact, concerns may be raised if you *don't* experience and display these sort of reactions following your loss.

Your Journey Through Stage 1—Acclimation and Adjustment

As you pass through Stage 1 of your grief journey, you move along a continuum that begins with your initial exposure to the death and the shock, avoidance, and denial that come immediately afterward. As you near the end of this first stage, you become acclimated to the loss. Only after you work through the initial trauma can you begin to move on to Stage 2.

Exposure   Acclimation

Stage 1: Acclimation and Adjustment

Adjusting to and Describing Your Loss

The first goal in your grief work is to accommodate your loss —find a way to accept it and begin adjusting to the changes it's brought to your life. This is an important early step; however, like most facets of grief work, it's sometimes easier said than done. Ultimately, there's no way to "fake" adjustment and no way around the pain that accompanies it. Your grief work at this stage largely centers around allowing the full impact of the death to sink in. A second important aspect of adjustment is finding a means for expressing your thoughts and feelings in a way that prevents you from becoming "stuck" in your current emotions.

Describing your feelings and the circumstances of the death will help you develop internal strength and provide a framework upon which your later grief work can build.

You must find a way to think and talk about your loss—to get these things "outside" of your head. The capacity to express thoughts and feelings is a critical component to recovery from any trauma. But you may not be ready to talk to others about the depth of your feelings. Or you may feel you have no one to tell or that others won't want to hear everything you have to say. It may also be true that you don't know what to say, or *how* to say it.

Much of *The Healing Journey Through Grief* is about developing your skills in self-reflection and expression. Even if you aren't comfortable sharing your thoughts or deepest feelings with others, the journal entries in this book allow you to have a "conversation" with yourself. You may well find that writing about these difficult emotional experiences will be cathartic—you can unburden yourself by putting words to your feelings and giving a voice to your thoughts.

The first step to managing difficult feelings and overcoming obstacles is to face them. In these earliest days of your adjustment, writing about your loss will help you to confront it and begin to take the reality of the death into your life. Describing your feelings and the circumstances of the death will help you develop internal strength and provide a framework upon which your later grief work can build.

THESE EARLY DAYS

Sentence "starts" are a good way to facilitate journal writing when you feel a little stuck. They provide a kick start to help you focus on your feelings and thoughts. They can be used as an outline tool—a way to identify the things that you want to explore further in writing. You can complete the sentence stem as you create it or return to it later when you're ready to complete your thought.

Take a few moments to think about the words that best describe your reactions, feelings, or thoughts. Then complete these sentence starts.

1. *When I learned of the death, I felt . . .* _____

_____

2. *My reaction to the death was to . . .* _____

_____

3. *After the death, I . . .* _____

_____

4. *Since the death, I haven't been able to . . .* _____

_____

5. *Since the death, I mostly feel . . .* _____

_____

Beginning with these sentence starts, describe your current feelings in more detail.

1. *When I think of the death, I . . .* _____

_____

_____

_____

2. *Since the death, my life has changed the most in that . . .* _____

_____

_____

_____

_____

3. *Since my loss, I find my life to be . . .* _____

_____

_____

_____

_____

4. Since the death, I most need . . . _____

_____

_____

_____

_____

_____

_____

Create five sentences starts of your own, using the sentence starts above as examples. Focus each start on some aspect of your feelings or thoughts since your loss. Then finish the sentence.

1. Your sentence start: _____ . . .

_____

2. Your sentence start: _____ . . .

_____

3. Your sentence start: _____ . . .

_____

4. Your sentence start: _____ . . .

_____

5. Your sentence start: _____ . . .

_____

Complete this final sentence start.

As I finish this entry, I . . . _____

_____

_____

_____

- Was it difficult to write about some of your loss experiences? Did the writing come easier than you thought it might, or was it hard to come up with the words? Was writing a positive, negative, or neutral experience?
- Did the writing prompt other thoughts, feelings, or reactions? If it did, what will you do with these?

Expressing Your Feelings

Why is it important to express feelings? Any time you pick up a book that deals with psychology or self-improvement, or you listen to a therapist on TV or in your own life, you hear the idea that it's important for you to express your feelings and put your thoughts into words. Why? Talking about things that bother or affect us doesn't change a thing in the world around us. In fact, it's not at all unusual to hear people ask "What is the point of talking about it, if talking about it doesn't change it?"

It's not that self-expression—talking about it—changes the world. It can't. But, self-expression has the power to change you and the way you see and experience the world. Putting your feelings into words gives them shape and meaning. It allows you to put your feelings and thoughts *into* the world around you, and by doing that you connect to your environment and the people in your life. This makes you more whole.

Once out of your head, words give meaning and clarity to your feelings and thoughts, and sometimes allow you to be relieved of them. To express means to press or squeeze out, to make known and reveal. Sometimes if you don't express, you explode. And the danger of such an explosion is particularly acute if you're dealing with something as devastating as the loss of a loved one. Expression allows you a sort of freedom—the freedom to recognize and overcome troubling feelings and thoughts. This out-

Self-expression has the power to change you and the way you see and experience the world.

pouring of feelings as you express them, and the relief this expression can bring from pain and anxiety, is called catharsis.

You don't need to understand what you're feeling in order to express it. You'll have plenty of time later to sort out the textures of your feelings and look at what's causing them. Right now, all you need to focus on is recognizing that you're having a feeling and putting it into words.

CHECKPOINT: ADJUSTMENT

1. How is what you're reading and thinking affecting the way you feel? *Right now I feel* . . .

_____

_____

_____

_____

2. Describe the ideas, opinions, and impressions that are going through your head. *Right now I'm thinking about* . . . _____

_____

_____

_____

_____

_____

3. *The thing that most keeps me from expressing myself is* . . . _____

_____

_____

_____

4. *What helps me give voice to my feelings is* . . . _____

_____

_____

THINGS TO THINK ABOUT

- Do you see a difference between a "thought" and a "feeling?" Can you easily distinguish between your thoughts and feelings?
- Do you understand the causes of your feelings and *why* you feel that way?
- Is there a connection between thoughts and feelings — does one affect the other?

Experiencing Your Loss

It's been said that "once bereaved, always bereaved." From that point of view, talking about "recovering" from grief is almost disrespectful, as life is never restored to the way it was before the loss of someone close. Of course, when people speak of recovery, they really refer to overcoming grief and adapting to life after the death. This is an important distinction to draw, because the purpose of grief is not to "get over" your loss but to adjust to its consequences and help you restore your balance.

The purpose of grief work is not to "get over" your loss but to adjust to its consequences and help you restore your balance.

Life changes after loss, and this is no doubt true for you. For some, the loss may be huge, tied to every aspect of your life; for others, although the loss may be peripheral to your daily life, nonetheless something has been torn away. The intensity of feeling associated with your loss—how deeply you mourn and for how long—is tied to your relationship with your loved one. The more intimately your lives were connected, the more likely it is that your grief will be intensely felt and your sense of loss profound.

The purely emotional aspects of your grief—the experience of absence and the sadness and sense of displacement that comes with your loss—are made even more complex if your lives were tied together in practical as well as emotional ways. If your loved one shared the responsibilities of parenting, generating income, or managing a household, your grief is further complicated by worry and anxiety about your ability to cope with practical reality.

But, despite the complications of a shared partnership, loss is measured by its emotional impact, not its practical consequences. Whether your loved one was also a working partner in your life or a family member or friend without any practical ties, the depths of your loss are gauged by the size of the emotional gap left in your life.

Expressing Your Loss

The point of *The Healing Journey Through Grief* is self-expression and, following that, reflection and recovery. This is surely why you're using it—as a tool to better understand and successfully work through your grief.

At this early stage in your mourning, the purpose of self-expression is not self-awareness. That is, for now, your task is not to understand—and certainly not to overcome—your feelings. Instead, the current task is to *experience* your feelings and learn to *express* them so that you don't get emotionally stuck as you move along your journey.

When you're feeling very emotional, your feelings and thoughts can race. It can be hard to know exactly how you feel or what you're thinking, because you're feeling everything at once. Often when people experience powerful emotions they only experience a *global* feeling—they feel sad, angry, or happy. Part of being able to express yourself, though, is learning to "isolate" some of your thoughts and feelings so that you think about, feel, and express different aspects of that "global" feeling. Your feeling of loss, too, has many parts to it, as does your ability to adjust to it.

Everyone has a different experience of loss. Your journal is one place to describe your experiences and tell *your* story. As you work through your grief journey, you'll be writing and working through the story of life at this difficult time. But this journey begins with *your* sad experience of loss. We know there is life after death—*your* life, after the death of your loved one. And this is where your adjustment must begin, at the beginning of this new part of your life.

In the entry that follows, rather than *generally* thinking about your loss, you'll focus on only one aspect of it. The entry will help you explore just one part of your feelings. For that reason you should repeat this entry, so you can think and write about different aspects of your loss.

THIS LOSS IN MY LIFE

1. What three things about your loss are on your mind right now?

a. _____

b. _____

c. _____

2. Which of these three things do you want to explore in this writing entry?

_____

3. Why do you want to write about this part of your loss?

_____

_____

4. How does this aspect of your loss make you feel?

_____

_____

5. What might help you better deal with this part of your loss?

_____

_____

6. What can you do to better adjust to or accept this part of your loss?

_____

_____

- Do you wonder if this part of your loss will ever change? Do you think it will?
- How do you feel as you work through this entry? Is writing about your loss difficult?

One of the advantages of recording your thoughts in your grief journal is that it gives you a chance to review and reflect on what you've written. Take a moment now to reread what you've just written and to think about it. Then write down any new thoughts that you may have about your loss or what you've written.

7. *Right now I feel . . .* _____

_____

_____

_____

THINGS TO THINK ABOUT

- Do you usually ever stop long enough in your daily routine to actually think about your life and what's weighing on your mind at that moment? What is it like to reflect on your life in this way?
- Will you use this entry again, to think about and express other aspects of your loss or any other feelings?

Barriers to Adjustment

You know already that loss is difficult for everyone. So too are the things that make it difficult to adjust to a loss. There may be many complicating issues in your life that make adjustment to this loss especially difficult.

Perhaps the circumstances of the death were particularly troubling. Or you may be shocked by the sudden burden of being a single parent. Or you may have to care for an infirm relative who is now alone. Being aware of barriers that make it particularly difficult for you to adjust is the first step to overcoming those obstacles.

BARRIERS

1. *The biggest change I've faced in my life since the death is . . .* _____

_____

_____

_____

_____

2. *The thing I'm having the most trouble adjusting to is . . .* _____

_____

_____

_____

3. *Three things that are interfering with my ability to adjust are . . .*

a. _____

b. _____

c. _____

4. *Some things I can do to help me get over these hurdles are . . .* _____

_____

_____

_____

_____

THINGS TO THINK ABOUT

- Were you able to recognize events, circumstances, or personal problems that are affecting your ability to adjust?
- Do you need special help to overcome special problems or obstacles to adjustment? If so, what kind of help—family, friends, clergy, counselor, support group?
- As you complete this chapter, reflect on the work you've done so far. Are you ready to move on to the next chapter, or do you need to do more work in this chapter?
- Do you feel committed to continue with your journaling?

4

Destination: ACCEPTANCE

"Melancholy and remorse form the deep leaden keel which enables us to sail into the wind of reality."
—CYRIL CONNOLLY

KATE

Georgia is a wonderful kid—she's bright and has always been full of life. But, I do worry about her since the death of her father—my son—eight months ago.

She's only ten and seems to be having such a difficult time with her grief. She often asks why her dad had to die, and if people who have died ever come back. She's less active now, and sometimes she says she doesn't want to do something because it would make her think of her father, or she wouldn't want to do that without her dad. She seems to think of him all the time, and sometimes she says things like, "Do you think Daddy will like this?" I worry that she hasn't been able to accept the death.

DANA

I'm having a really hard time accepting his death. I certainly haven't been able to adjust to it—I haven't changed a thing in the apartment. I haven't taken down any of his photos or put away any or his clothing or possessions. I really don't want to, and I certainly haven't thought about how I'll manage without him.

At work, I never talk about what's happened. I think people think I'm weird because I don't. With family and friends, they know I don't want to think about it, so they avoid talking about him. And when I'm alone I use wine a lot, so I can sort of feel emotionally numb to it all, and don't have to deal with it. I just can't believe he's dead.

ADJUSTMENT IS NOT the same thing as acceptance. Adjustment is a response to change and involves accommodating that change. But adjustment doesn't mean *accepting* the change. It may not always be desirable to accept something, even though you have to adjust to it. For instance, you may have to adjust to a serious illness, but you don't have to give in to it. You may have to adjust to social values you don't agree with, but you can work to change them. As opposed to adjustment, acceptance of something means that you're not fighting the new reality—you're acknowledging and acquiescing to it. In the case of your loss, you *must* accept it. You must give in to the reality of the death, because all of your feelings, your regrets, and your behaviors cannot change it. In your grief work, you can only change yourself.

Adjustment is a response to change and involves accommodating that change. But adjustment doesn't mean accepting *the change.*

Accepting the Change

Accepting will mean different things at different points in your bereavement. At this early stage of your grief, accepting requires only that you *acknowledge* the reality of the death and accept the changes in your life. Later, accepting will mean *submitting* to your feelings and accepting their power. As you work through the final stages of your grief, accepting means *concession*—your willingness to fully accept the loss and move on.

In many ways, acceptance really underpins adjustment. To more fully adjust, you have to really work on accepting death and the changes it's brought.

What sort of things help people accept death? The memorials and customs that follow the immediate loss play several important roles. Funerals, spiritual services, and commemorative gatherings make death very concrete, which is one important part of acceptance. They also provide an opportunity for people to vent their feelings and display their emotions. Eulogies and other spoken memorials allow the bereaved to formally say their good-byes. Unspoken tributes like flowers allow a symbolic good-bye. The family gatherings that often take place after the funeral allow the mourners to give and receive condolences, talk and exchange memories, and vent emotions among people closest to them. Each of these customs contains the wisdom of folklore and serves a number of healing functions.

Family gatherings that often take place after the funeral allow the mourners to give and receive condolences, talk and exchange memories, and vent emotions among people closest to them.

+ They make death very real.

+ They remind you that although the body of your loved one has passed, the spirit and memory live on in *your* life.

+ They allow a way to formally say good-bye.

+ They provide a public recognition of your loss.

+ They provide the opportunity to openly display and vent emotions.

+ They allow the burden of death to be shared with other mourners.

+ They allow you to get emotional support from others.

+ They allow you to give emotional support to others.

+ They give you the chance to reminisce and to talk specifically about your loss and generally about your loved one with others.

+ They give your support group a chance to see how you're doing over the first days and to gauge whether more support or help is needed.

RITE OF PASSAGE

1. What was the funeral like for you?

_____

_____

_____

_____

_____

2. What words were spoken that affected or inspired you?

_____

_____

_____

_____

3. What other aspects of the funeral affected you?

_____

_____

_____

_____

4. What was the most moving and memorable part of the ceremony?

_____

_____

_____

_____

_____

5. Take a few moments to think back on the funeral. Think about it deeply. Remember what the weather was like that day and the way you felt. Try to recall the *mood* of the ceremony, and briefly describe it.

_____

_____

_____

_____

_____

_____

_____

6. Describe the ceremony again, focusing on its most moving aspects.

_____

_____

_____

_____

_____

7. Are there any words that should have been said at the funeral, but were not? If there are, say them now.

_____

_____

_____

_____

_____

_____

Acceptance and Expression

Self-expression comes in many forms. Words, spoken and written, are probably our most common form of self-expression—most people have spoken or written about their feelings at some point in their lives. Written self-expressions can come in many forms from prose to poetry, and everything in between. Words can also be used to express feelings through song. Spoken self-expressions are the foundation for psychotherapy, which is based on the idea that emotions can be vented through talking, thereby restoring balance.

There are plenty of forms of self-expression that don't use words at all. For instance, although most journals are written, there are also sketch pad journals for those who prefer drawing or painting. Dance and music are other nonverbal ways to project and express internal feelings out into the world.

The ability to be self-expressive is an important component of accepting change.... The idea is that ridding yourself of excess emotional energy is healthy and helps you adapt and get through life without exploding under pressure.

The ability to be self-expressive is an important component of accepting change. You probably know this already—people are often encouraged to "vent," get rid of their "baggage," or "let off steam." The idea is that ridding yourself of excess emotional energy is healthy and helps you adapt and get through life without exploding under pressure. Writing about your loss can also help you discharge some of your feelings. It serves to "concretize" the death and make it real. And as you translate your thoughts and feelings to paper, you can sometimes get them out of your head.

I STILL CAN'T BELIEVE IT

There may be times where you find yourself shaking your head, saying, "I still can't believe it." There is nothing wrong with that thought; it's completely normal and may go on for a while. At some point, you'll notice a change from "I can't believe this *is* happening," to "I can't believe this *has* happened." That will mark the point at which you've begun to fully accept the reality of your loss and are moving through your bereavement.

1. How has your world changed since the death?

_____

_____

_____

_____

2. What do you especially miss?

_____

_____

_____

3. What's the hardest thing to accept?

_____

_____

_____

4. What's it like when you realize this really *has* happened?

_____

_____

_____

5. What makes you the maddest?

_____

_____

_____

- Does writing or talking help? If it does, in what ways? If it doesn't, are there other ways you can express yourself?
- Do you have lots of thoughts and feelings about the death which you've not yet expressed? If so, how are you going to discharge these feelings? Do you want to?

Narrating the Death

"Take this sorrow to thy heart, and make it a part of thee, and it shall nourish thee until thou art strong again."
—HENRY WADSWORTH LONGFELLOW

Everyone is different. Some people are comfortable talking about the source of the death. Others would rather avoid the subject completely.

Every journal is different also, but common to many is the descriptive entry that tells the story of an event. In this case, that event is the death of your loved one. Why talk about the death at all? This death has been important in your life or has affected you in some way; otherwise, you likely wouldn't be reading and working through this book.

Many believe that retelling a story is healing, because in the telling comes an unburdening of tension. And, as you become more and more distant in time from the actual death, the stories you write about it will become an important chronicle of this part of your life.

REMEMBERING THE DAY

For some, the very act of recounting a traumatic event can trigger all sorts of emotional reactions. You should proceed with caution if the story of this death is especially traumatic for you. You'll know this as soon as you start to work on your entry or even as you begin thinking about it. If it produces unbearable feelings, then you're not yet ready to write about the death. Come back to the entry at a later time, and make sure you have someone to talk to if you find that your entry is especially troubling to you.

1. What were the day and date of the death?

_____

2. What can you remember about the rest of that day? What was the weather like? Was there a significant event in the news? How was your everyday life going before you heard the news? What were the details of the day?

_____

_____

_____

_____

_____

_____

_____

_____

_____

_____

3. Where were you when you learned of the death? What were you doing?

_____

_____

_____

_____

_____

_____

_____

_____

_____

_____

4. What led up to this loss? Write the story of the death.

_____

_____

_____

_____

_____

_____

_____

_____

_____

_____

_____

_____

_____

5. Did you get a chance to say good-bye?

_____

_____

6. If you could have spoken to your loved one that day, what would you have said? If you did speak that day, what would you now add?

_____

_____

_____

_____

- Was if useful to think and write about the death and to revisit it through the telling of the story? Are there other stories of the death you want to tell?
- Is it important to chronicle these events? Will it be better for you to write these stories down and keep them so that you can return to them at a later time, or are these stories you want to pass on to others and leave untold in writing?

If you decide that it's important or useful to chronicle other events and circumstances in the days before your loss, use this type of entry to focus on one day or a specific event. Your journal can then really help you to hone in on the details that make up your life and your grief.

I CHOOSE TO OVERCOME GRIEF

"Grant me the serenity to accept the things I cannot change, the courage to change the things I can, and the wisdom to know the difference."——REINHOLD NIEBUHR

I. Complete this thought by checking off the description that most resonates for you, and complete the sentence. You can also add one or two of your own sentence starts.

My grief feels like . . .

the seasons coming and going because . . . _____

_____

a complicated puzzle because . . . _____

_____

physical pain because . . . _____

_____

a broken vase because . . . _____

_____

a raging river because . . . _____

_____

Your sentence start: _____

because . . . _____

Your sentence start: _____

because . . . _____

2. Complete this sentence. *I choose to overcome my grief because . . .* _____

_____

_____

_____

_____

3. "Will's and won'ts" represent your commitment to stay emotionally and physically healthy. Think about each one before you check off your agreement.

a. __ I *will* stay active in my daily life.

b. __ I *will* be patient with myself.

c. __ I *will* connect with others.

d. __ I *will* express my feelings.

e. __ I *will* take care of my physical health.

f. __ I *will* seek support if I need it.

a. __ I *won't* expect people to know how I'm feeling if I don't tell them.

b. __ I *won't* try to hide my feelings.

c. __ I *won't* try to predict how long it will take to feel better.

d. __ I *won't* isolate myself.

e. __ I *won't* make any major decisions.

f. __ I *won't* try to escape from my feelings.

THINGS TO THINK ABOUT

- Was it difficult to agree to the "will's and won'ts"? Are you really ready to follow their suggestions as you work your way through grief?
- Reread the "will's and won'ts" periodically to remind yourself of your commitment to stay emotionally and physically healthy.
- Have you been able to accept your loss? What has been the most helpful thing in helping you to accept? What has been the most difficult part of acceptance?

5

Destination:
SUPPORT

PAUL

Elizabeth died after a long illness, and I suddenly felt really alone in the world. Of course, I wasn't alone because we had two young children, but it was hard to find solace in anything, including the kids. I know I had to make it through this really tough time, not only for myself but for their sake—losing their mom was hard enough on the kids without losing me to my depression.

Being a single parent was really difficult. Even though I'd been taking care of them alone throughout Elizabeth's illness, she was still there to give them emotional care and to give me her perspective and her support. After she passed away, I realized how important it had been to get support and help throughout the illness, and especially now. I'd been given lots of help by Elizabeth's family, our friends, and even neighbors, and thankfully the help was still coming. The practical help with the kids and housekeeping gave me time to spend on my own mourning, and the emotional support made it clear that it was okay to take care of myself as well.

47

That support was important in lots of ways. If helped me take care of those parts of my life that hadn't *changed—like meeting the physical needs of the kids. It also provided me with the space and time for my own grief so that I could find the strength I needed to meet the emotional needs of the kids. Over time, of course, my needs for help have changed, but the comfort, support, and practical help provided by friends got me—and the kids—through a very difficult time in our lives. Without that support, things could have easily gone another way.*

ONE OF THE most conspicuous elements in most mourning ceremonies is the support mustered and caring displayed for the bereaved. People are expected to come to the assistance of those who have lost someone close and are reckoned upon as the first and most immediate level of support for the bereaved. Not everyone will have available for them this level of support, though, and for the bereaved the task is made that much harder.

There are many levels of support—from the concerned attitude of work colleagues to the shared grief and solace by close family members and friends. Because support comes from different sources, and is offered for different reasons, it varies widely in its intensity and ability to provide comfort and care. For instance, you wouldn't expect a work colleague to spend his or her evenings with you in the days or weeks following your loss, but you might reasonably expect a close friend or family member to do just that.

You'll need much support in your bereavement—of different types, at different times, and from different people. In this chapter, you'll have the chance to think about the kind of support that is available in your life and where it comes from. Perhaps most important, the journal entries in this chapter will help you to understand the kind of help *you* want and need, and how to get it.

Sources of Support

You have two kinds of support systems. The first is a "natural" support system group made up of family, friends, and others in your daily life. Your natural support group consists of your "inner" circle of close relatives, friends, and others and an "outer" circle of neighbors, coworkers, and more distant friends. Natural support stems from your family and others in your daily life and is an *automatic* response to your loss—people will naturally provide support without your having to seek it out.

You also have available to you a "drafted" support system, which must be developed. Drafted support includes all help that must be sought out—usually because the natural support system can't meet your emotional, financial, or practical needs. People in your natural support system are, by definition, in your life and can see your loss for themselves. Their support flows from this awareness. However, drafted supporters are unaware of your loss until you tell them. Drafted support is not any less well meaning or sincere than natural support, but it's a different level and type of support, and it has to be activated by someone. The distinction between natural and drafted support is akin to the difference between first aid delivered on the spot by someone present at the time of the injury and treatment provided by medical practitioners who must be notified of the injury.

It's important to know that you have both types of support available and also how to distinguish between the two. It's of equal importance that you understand which type of support you need, and how to get it.

Types of Support

There are many types of support, meeting different needs. The types of support can be divided into two main categories: emotional support and practical support.

You have two kinds of support systems. The first is a "natural" support system group. . . . You also have available to you a "drafted" support system.

- *Words of sympathy*. This is the kind of natural support that you get from friends, neighbors, and colleagues and sometimes even from places least expected. It's a level of social support and concern that you're never likely to have to ask for.

- *Companionship*. You'll typically get this kind of support from closer friends and family members. Sometimes all that's required is to have someone nearby.

- *Someone to talk to*. This goes beyond companionship and touches on the need for self-expression and the opportunity to be relieved of some of your thoughts, feelings, and concerns.

- *Connection*. This type of support fills the need for "belonging" and provides a sense of connection to something permanent like a family. Your bereavement may be especially frightening if you fear that the death will eventually cut you off from the family of your loved one.

- *Sharing*. This is a level of support often found within families, but it can also come from other places, such as grief support groups. This type of support provides the chance to share your grief with others going through the same experience. Through grief support groups, you can get advice, gather hope and inspiration from others who are successfully handling their own grief, and build relationships that may last beyond your grief work.

- *Advice and counseling*. Despite their best and most sincere wishes, supporters often don't know what to say or how to help you through a grief process that may be overwhelming at times. If you find you need more help than the people in your support group can provide, or you feel unable to share with them, you should think about talking to a caregiver who's trained to help. You can turn to your primary care physician, minister, or other professional caregiver such as a therapist, social worker, psychologist, or pastoral counselor.

PRACTICAL SUPPORT

* *Physical help.* Many times, supporters directly help out with the cooking and other physical chores during and after the funeral and in some cases for a period of time afterward. Although useful, this sort of support is usually short-lived. If the bereaved are elderly or infirm, physical help may have to be provided on a more ongoing basis. Sometimes this will involve drafting help, by securing the aid of in-home housekeeping or nursing services. Other ongoing needs for physical support might include childcare help if there are young children in the home of a newly widowed parent.

* *Financial help.* This is an often awkward, but possibly critical, area in which very concrete support may be needed after a loss.

* *Organizational and planning assistance.* You may need legal help, financial counseling, or other forms of practical help to help you figure out how to manage your life and handle any special complications that the death may have created.

* *Keeping anchored.* Supporters who know you well will be able to see how you're doing and help you keep on target. Even though there's an emotional part to this sort of support, it's a very practical form of help where the focus is to ensure that you're okay.

THE DAY AFTER

Support is probably the most active, and the least organized, in the immediate aftermath of the death. Family, friends, neighbors, coworkers, and others in your natural support system are quick to respond and eager to help console you and lighten your burden. The most useful kinds of immediate support include *practical* help with the daily aspects of your life—looking after the children, walking the dog, and paying the bills—and *emotional* support—simply being there.

What was the day after like for you? What kind of support did you get, and how did it feel? Did it ease the pain and help get you through the day?

1. What sort of support did you most immediately need during the first day and the day after?

_____

_____

_____

_____

2. Who was most important in providing support the next day? Who stands out, and why?

_____

_____

_____

_____

3. Was it important to receive support the next day? If it was, why?

_____

_____

_____

_____

4. What aspect of that support are you most grateful for?

_____

_____

_____

_____

_____

_____

THINGS TO THINK ABOUT

- What would the next day have been like if you hadn't received support?
- Did you get the kind of support you needed? If you didn't get as much or the kind of support needed, why not?
- Are you still getting support, and is it the kind of support you want and need?
- Do you know what kind of support you need?

Support over Time

Your practical and emotional support isn't going to end with the passing of the first few days. In face, your need for support will almost certainly increase over time, although the type of support you'll need is likely to change.

As your needs change in the days and weeks that follow the death, you shouldn't have to ask for support or educate people about your pain and the practical and emotional difficulties you might be facing. Nevertheless, not everyone gets the kind of help and support they need following a loss.

There are many reasons for a lack of support. Some people live a life that's relatively isolated and without support to begin with. In a situation like this, death just brings further isolation. In other cases, the bereaved may feel uncomfortable with support and give helpers the message that they're not really necessary.

Your need for practical and emotional support isn't going to end with the passing of the first few days. In fact, your need for support will almost certainly increase over time, although the type of support you'll need is likely to change.

Being honest about your feelings may sometimes make you feel like you're criticizing others or being ungrateful, but you're not—it's just a description of the way you feel.

Some people feel they shouldn't *need* help, and others may feel too proud to ask for comfort and support. Under any circumstances, after a few days the initial flurry and show of support usually diminishes, and life returns to normal for your supporters. They may not realize that life hasn't returned to normal for *you,* or that you still need help and support. Or they may know you need help but not know what kind of support to provide or how to give it.

Your pain may go unnoticed, especially by people outside of your immediate circle. People expect you to recover from grief, and they may not see how much you're still hurting. As time passes, the level of support you receive will diminish. Right or wrong, people will expect you to be "getting over" it. In fact, unless your display of grief is so clear—through depression, obvious changes in behavior, episodes of crying, or other public displays of grief—many will assume you're doing just fine. Most people won't know how you're doing, or even realize you still need help, especially if you seem to be doing okay. Understand that few people will know what you actually need, unless you tell them. Don't expect them to read your mind—"They should *know* how I'm feeling," or "You should *know* how much this still hurts." Most people *don't* know, and if you don't let them know they never will.

Accordingly, and increasingly over time, you'll have to know what support you need, how to get it, and who to get it from.

THE RIGHT HELP AT THE RIGHT TIME

Your journal will be of the most use to you when you use it honestly. Sometimes this may mean thinking and writing about a difficult subject that requires a frank appraisal of yourself or someone else. Remember that your journal is a private place to enter your thoughts and experiences; it need never be shared. Being honest about your feelings may sometimes make you feel like you're criticizing others or being ungrateful, but you're not—it's just a description of the way you feel. Your job in this journal entry, as with all others, is to be totally honest about your feelings.

1. Is the sort of support you're currently receiving the sort of support you need or want? Why?

_____

_____

_____

_____

_____

_____

_____

2. What kind of support do you most need?

_____

_____

_____

_____

_____

_____

_____

3. What kind of support do you least want?

_____

_____

_____

_____

_____

_____

_____

4. Describe your three greatest *practical* needs at this time.

a. _____

b. _____

c. _____

5. Name your three greatest *emotional* needs.

a. _____

b. _____

c. _____

6. Are the people in your support system accurately recognizing your needs? If not, why not?

_____

_____

_____

_____

_____

7. What do you need to do in order to get the sort of support you really want?

_____

_____

_____

_____

- Are your needs being recognized? If not, what's getting in the way?
- Is your need for support changing as time passes? Do you need a different kind of support now from the support you needed in the days immediately after the death?
- Are you using the support you have, or are you creating your own obstacles to getting support?

Matching Support to Needs

You probably have a clearer sense by now of what your needs for help look like and the areas where you need the greatest support. Do you also have a sense of where this support can come from? In all walks of life and all sorts of situations, people sometimes set themselves up for failure. They have expectations that cannot be met; they seek attention from the wrong people; they ask for what they cannot have. Looking to the wrong places from unattainable things leads to disappointment and dissatisfaction.

To get support and help, you have to know where to look for it. It's not that people don't want to help, but asking the *right* people for the *wrong* kind of help—that is, help they can't provide—is bound to make them feel inadequate and may leave you feeling alone, uncared for, or bitter.

As you consider your needs, match them to the people in your support system. What sort of help can be provided by different people within your natural support system, and what sort of help can you reasonably expect? For instance, you're more likely to be able to count on your sister for child care than a neighbor or work colleague. On the other hand, your need for privacy and quiet solitude is more likely to be honored by coworkers than by immediate family members. Or you might have to step completely out of your natural support system and seek drafted support, such as the help offered by a grief counselor or the affinity offered by other participants in a grief support group.

To get support and help, you have to know where to look for it. . . . As you consider your needs, match them to the people in your support system.

RECOGNIZING SUPPORT

1. What sort of people are available to you for support? Your strongest natural support group typically includes those people in your daily life who know you best (i.e., those in your inner circle). The support provided by people in your outer circle is likely to be more limited, less intense, and relatively short-lived.

   Usually you have to seek out "drafted" support—help outside of your natural system. But you may already have such support in your life if, for example, you participate in a grief counseling group, see a therapist, or frequently talk to your minister or rabbi. If these types of supporters are already in your life, think of them as part of your natural support system.

2. Check off or list the types of support currently available to you.

Type of Support	Natural Support _Inner Circle_	Natural Support _Outer Circle_	Drafted Support
Clergy	—	—	—
Close friends	—	—	—
Coworkers	—	—	—
Counseling support group	—	—	—
Counselor/Therapist	—	—	—
Family physician	—	—	—
Family therapist	—	—	—
Home health care	—	—	—
Housekeeping	—	—	—
Immediate family	—	—	—
In-laws	—	—	—
Neighbors	—	—	—
School officials (for parents)	—	—	—
School officials (for students)	—	—	—

Type of Support	Natural Support *Inner Circle*	Natural Support *Outer Circle*	Drafted Support
Teachers	—	—	—
Work supervisor	—	—	—
_____	—	—	—
_____	—	—	—
_____	—	—	—
_____	—	—	—
_____	—	—	—

3. You just checked off *groups* of people who are available to you for support. Now think of five specific people from the inner and outer circles of your natural support group that you can turn to for support and help. Write their names in the spaces provided.

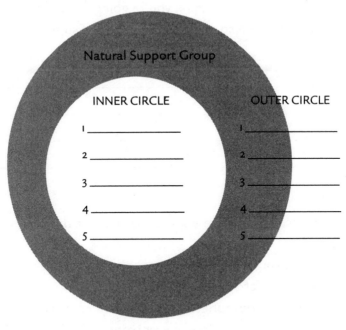

Natural Support Group

INNER CIRCLE

1 _____
2 _____
3 _____
4 _____
5 _____

OUTER CIRCLE

1 _____
2 _____
3 _____
4 _____
5 _____

Support Systems

4. Think about the kinds of needs you named in your previous journal entry. Can any of the people named above provide you with the kind of help or support you've identified?

_____

_____

_____

_____

_____

5. Do these people know the kind of support you need from them? How do they know?

_____

_____

_____

_____

_____

6. At this point in your grief, do you think you're going to have to draft some additional support and assistance? If so, describe what kind of support you will need.

_____

_____

_____

_____

_____

THINGS TO THINK ABOUT

- Do you see a difference between help and support? Is it difficult to ask for either help or support?
- Do you ever worry that your support will "dry up" over time or that people will expect you to get over your grief?
- Do you use your support appropriately? Do you underuse your support, do you take your support for granted, or do you ever wonder if you depend too much on your support?

Support and Help in Your Life

By now, you've thought a lot about support and help. You may have decided that the level of support you are currently getting fits your needs. Or you may have found that your present support system isn't at all adequate. The goal here is for you to understand the role of support in your life and then decide what it *should* be and what it actually *is*. Once you've decided how important support is to you, and whether your needs match the support you are getting, you'll be in a position to more actively get your needs met.

Is there a difference between help and support? Although the words are often used interchangeably, "help" suggests a direct activity, in which your supporters are *doing* things for you—*help*ing out. This could be shopping for you, taking care of your house, or driving you to an appointment. Of course, in each of these examples, the help provided *is* support. But "support" more generally refers to emotional activity, such as offering sympathy, talking and encouraging, listening, and just being there for you. As you complete this next entry, think about the difference between support and help. Each time you see either word, think about your reactions to both words.

CHECKPOINT: SUPPORT

1. How can you tell when you need support or help?

_____

_____

_____

_____

_____

_____

2. When you need support, do you seek it out?

_____

_____

_____

_____

_____

_____

3. When offered support, do you accept it?

_____

_____

_____

_____

4. Name five things that interfere with your willingness to let people know you need support or help or with your ability to accept it when offered.

a. _____

b. _____

c. _____

d. _____

e. _____

5. Whose help have you accepted, and whose help haven't you accepted? Why?

_____

_____

_____

_____

_____

_____

6. Write a few words on the place of support and help in your life right now.

_____

_____

_____

_____

_____

_____

_____

THINGS TO THINK ABOUT

- Do you feel you have a pretty clear sense of the kind of support you need, the kind of support you have, and how to get support?
- What have you learned about your needs? What have you learned about the role of support in your life at this time?
- Is this a journal entry to repeat again after some time has passed? In what ways do you think your needs for support and help will change over time?

6

Destination: SHARING

BARRY

Nan had a long struggle before she died, and three remissions. But after several cancers, she eventually died of a brain tumor. It wasn't a huge surprise to know that Nan was going to pass away, after all those bouts, but the inevitability of her death didn't make it any easier for me or our two daughters.

One of the things that's helped the kids is the support they have at school. They've joined a support group there for kids who have lost a parent, and it's been great that they've got a place where they can share this terrible experience with other kids who're going through the same thing, and a grief counselor who's running the group. But after a while, I realized the kids also needed to share with me, not just their group.

For me, it was a little harder to share. I felt like I had to keep it together for the children, and I didn't tell many people how I was really feeling. But watching the kids, I realized that the best way for me to help them was to help myself. Seeing how much the school group was helping to relieve their pressure made me realize that I needed to share my feelings also. I've since become more outgoing

"It is comforting when one has a sorrow to lie in the warmth of one's bed and there, abandoning all effort and all resistance, to bury even one's head under the cover, giving one's self up to it completely, moaning like branches in the autumn wind. But there is still a better bed, full of divine odors. It is our sweet, our profound, our impenetrable friendship."

—MARCEL PROUST

with my feelings, which has definitely helped. It's also been easier for me to listen to and share with the kids.

YOUR LOSS ITSELF is probably quite dislocating. You've not only lost someone very important to you, but you may also feel wrenched apart from an important and stable part of your life that helped define your identity and shape your future. In other words, your relationship with your loved one may have provided a connection and direction that went beyond the relationship itself.

Because the experience of grief can be so dislocating, it's particularly difficult when your loss isn't shared with others. About this, the early Roman epigrammatist Martial said, "He truly sorrows who sorrows unseen." A sense of belonging and being connected to a community is very important as you move through the grieving process. You need to feel like part of something while grieving.

In Chapter 5, you thought and wrote about getting support. But that's only one aspect of community and connection. *Sharing* the experience is something quite different. Bereavement support is often a one-way street flowing from the community to you. Sharing is more of a two-way street—a mutual experience of exchange as you share with others and they share with you.

A sense of belonging and being connected to a community is very important as you move through the grieving process.

The Relationship as an "Anchor"

Who are you without your relationship? If you are a widowed spouse or romantic partner, you may feel less than whole now; it may seem as though half your life has simply vanished. If you've lost a parent, how you feel will depend on your age and your relationship with your deceased parent. As an adult child, you may feel that you've lost an "anchoring" point in your life—a parent who was always simply *there* as a symbol of permanence or who served as the head of your extended family. It isn't uncommon for even middle-aged adult children to experience a sense of orphanhood. Of course, for a child or adolescent, the loss of a parent is devastating. The parent was probably a daily provider of needs varying from love to nurturance to guidance to emotional and financial security.

If you're a bereaved parent, the loss of your child is stunning and earth-shattering. No matter how old your lost child—whether an infant or an adult—you simply don't expect to outlive your child, and you may feel empty and guilty. If you've lost a sibling or close friend, your loss experience is different again, but the outcome may once again shatter not only your sense of the world but your sense of place in that world too.

The issues of loss and its impact on your own sense of self are big ones. In this chapter, you'll work on your sense of loss through your connection with your community. In later chapters, you'll continue to explore these issues by focusing on dealing with your feelings, finding new meaning, and rebuilding your personal identity and social relationships.

*I measure every Grief
I meet with narrow,
probing Eyes—I
wonder if It weighs like
Mine—Or has an
Easier size.*
— EMILY DICKINSON

Sharing and Support

In the previous chapter, you focused on support—its meaning, where to get it, and how best to use it. In this chapter, the focus is on sharing. Sharing is just another face of support—and both require and involve community.

- Support implies community—a group of people to whom you can turn when you need help. When you share, you share with others in that same community.

- To get support, you have to share. You're not likely to get support unless you've shared your loss and needs.

- Although support after bereavement is often one-way (usually, you receive support), both support and sharing can go in either direction or both. You can get support or give it; you can share and be shared with.

Perhaps this last aspect is the most critical. Support and sharing can move only in one direction, or they can be *mutual* processes. You can give and take at the same time.

The Faces of Sharing

Sharing can support and strengthen you in your bereavement, and it can help to link you with others.

Sharing serves different purposes at different times. At this time, sharing can support and strengthen you in your bereavement, and it can help to link you with others. Sharing with others can relieve your feelings and allow you to distribute your load among others who can help carry you through this difficult time. Sharing allows you to talk and reminisce about your loved one with others who also cared for the deceased. Perhaps as important, sharing allows others to communicate their bereavement to you—you are almost certainly not the only one affected deeply by this loss. Others may need your help, your comfort and consolation, and your support. So sharing brings your community together.

THE FACES OF YOUR SHARING

1. Check off all the ways of sharing that are typical for you.

_____ Letting people know when I need emotional help

_____ Being with others when *I* need some company

_____ Being with others when *they* need some company

_____ Letting others know about the problems I face managing my daily tasks

_____ Telling people about my practical worries, like financial stressors

_____ Reminiscing with others and sharing *my* stories and memories

_____ Reminiscing with others and sharing *their* stories and memories

_____ Sharing special events and commemorations with others in my community

_____ Sharing decisions and future plans

Other: _____

_____

_____

_____

2. In which three ways are you most likely to share with others?

a. _____

b. _____

c. _____

3. What are the three most difficult things to share?

a. _____

b. _____

c. _____

4. Do you share different things with different people? If you do, briefly describe them.

_____

_____

_____

_____

_____

THINGS TO THINK ABOUT

- Is there a pattern to the kind of sharing you do? Is there a pattern to the kind of sharing you don't do?
- What most motivates your willingness or need to share with others?
- Do you share enough? Are there things you ought to be sharing, but aren't?

What Is "Community?"

Sharing requires someone to share *with,* but simply knowing people doesn't mean you feel comfortable sharing anything with them. A grouping of people doesn't necessarily make a community. In a community, you experience sharing, collective purpose, and mutually satisfying interactions. By definition, communities share something in common.

In communities, different needs get met and different tasks accomplished. In a death, the community task is helping those who are bereaved through their grief. This includes you, of course, but probably includes others also. Some in your community may share your loss and the depth of your grief, although perhaps in different ways. For instance, if you've lost a sibling, it's likely that other brothers or sisters share your grief. Others in your community may not directly share your loss, but they are there for *you.* These two groups, those who grieve also and those who are there to support you, make up both ends of the grief community.

Your needs aren't so simple that you have only *one* type of want or that you need to share only *one* part of your life. Sharing fully means being able to express and communicate *all* your needs, not just some of them. You may know people with whom you share certain things but not others. For instance, you may be willing to tell someone that you're sad and miss your loved one, but you may not be willing (or able) to tell them that you're really having difficulties looking after the children or facing financial hardship. In a community, different people have different roles to fill, and no one person can complete all tasks or meet all needs.

Being able to share fully means being able to open up about feelings, thoughts, needs, decisions, and memories. You may not be able to share *all* of these needs with any single person; you'll need to turn to different people for different things. If there are

Being able to share fully means being able to open up about feelings, thoughts, needs, decisions, and memories. You may not be able to share all these needs with any single person; you'll need to turn to different people for different things.

few people in your community you can turn to, or no one you can really open up to, then your community is probably limited. You need to start thinking about how to open up and widen your support, and at the same time take note of who in the community can count on *you*.

THE FACES OF YOUR COMMUNITY

1. Who's in your community? With whom can you share?

_____

_____

_____

_____

_____

_____

2. Of these people, who do you feel most comfortable sharing with?

a. _____

b. _____

c. _____

d. _____

e. _____

f. _____

3. Do you share similar things with each person, or different things? Briefly expand on your answer.

_____

_____

_____

_____

4. Does your community meet all, or just some, of your needs?

_____

_____

_____

_____

_____

5. Are there others in your community who are expressing their own deep grief for this loss? Who?

_____

_____

_____

_____

6. What connection do you feel with others in your community whose grief is similar to your own?

_____

_____

_____

_____

THINGS TO THINK ABOUT

- Does your community meet your needs, or do you need to think about expanding your community's ability to meet your needs? How can you do this?
- Who needs to share with you, and what sort of things? Are you "tuned in" to the kind of help that others may need from you?

The Gift of Sharing

Through the sharing of feelings and ideas, you have the ability to communicate with others, to describe your grief and understand theirs, and to exchange comfort and solace. But unlike support, which you will usually only need when things are difficult, sharing is a vehicle to communicate and express both grief and joy and everything in between. As you work through your grief, you'll also find moments of pleasure and warmth. These are the gifts of sharing and part of the healing process that—although it may not seem like it—begins immediately.

How does sharing help? It's just one more form of expression, and you already know how that can help, or you wouldn't be keeping this grief journal. The difference between sharing and what you're doing right now—reading and writing in your journal—is that sharing has an *outward* nature whereas journaling involves *inward* reflection. Sharing means just that—participating in a community. And, through that form of outward contact, you *become* outward as you share your burden and join with something outside of yourself.

Unlike support, which you will usually only need when things are difficult, sharing is a vehicle to communicate and express both grief and joy and everything in between.

THE GIFT OF SHARING

1. What have you shared about your loss, needs, or decisions, and to whom?

_____

_____

_____

_____

_____

_____

_____

2. What are the *most* important things for you to share?

_____

_____

_____

_____

3. Have you shared these things? If you have, was it useful and do you need to share more? If you haven't been able to share, what's getting in the way?

_____

_____

_____

_____

_____

4. Who shares with you? What sort of things are shared with you?

_____

_____

_____

_____

_____

5. Who *needs* to share with you? Who needs your support, and in what ways?

_____

_____

_____

_____

_____

6. Are you pretty well tuned in to the needs of others? If you've been able to meet those needs, has it helped you to help them?

_____

_____

_____

_____

_____

_____

THINGS TO THINK ABOUT

- Have you shared enough with others? Has sharing helped?
- Do you need to share more or in different ways?
- Do you need to be more aware of the sort of support others may need from you?
- Do you need to reach out to people who may need you? Is it, or will it be, difficult to meet the needs of others?

Sharing and Journaling

Journaling is a highly personal form of communication, in the sense that you're really talking to *yourself* when you write. As effective and powerful as writing and drawing are as a means of reflection and expression, they are just one part of your recovery, not the whole thing. Sharing with others, and joining your community, is another.

Although journaling isn't sharing, it can grow as a jumping-off point for exchange. You might allow others to read your journal. Or you may read parts of it aloud to others. Or you may be prompted to discuss some of what you've learned through your journal. In each case, you're in communication with someone else, and that's what makes it sharing.

CHECKPOINT: SHARING

1. As you complete this chapter, how do you see your present community?

_____

_____

_____

_____

_____

2. Which of your needs are outside of the scope of your present community? Why are they?

_____

_____

_____

_____

_____

3. Do you need to expand your community, or is it meeting your needs as it is? If the former, how might you expand it?

_____

_____

_____

_____

_____

4. What four things could you do to expand your community?

a. _____

b. _____

c. _____

d. _____

5. What would be one supportive or sharing activity that would be of help to your community?

_____

_____

_____

_____

THINGS TO THINK ABOUT

- Where are the limits of self-expression through journaling? In what ways do you need to *directly* communicate with others and share?
- Are there parts of your journal that you can share with someone else? Who, and why?
- Do you need to be especially aware of anything in your community, about your own or anyone else's needs?

7

Destination:

UNDERSTANDING FEELINGS

ROB

There were plenty of times when my feelings got the better of me, and not just right after my brother died. I was really tied to Nick—he was only a year younger than me, but I was always like his mentor and his protector. When he died, I felt like I'd let him down because I couldn't protect him. And I really missed him.

But my feelings just wouldn't go away. At first, I was sad a lot and cried sometimes when I was alone. But, after a while I started to cut myself off from my friends in school—I didn't really know why. I just didn't want to be with anyone else. Then I started to get easily irritated with people and sort of pushed them away. Sometimes I'd snap at someone at home or in school. I got mean. After my mom and dad talked to me, I realized that I was feeling mad all the time, and had been since Nick died. I just didn't know it till then.

I think my guilt was what hurt the most and made things really bad for me, like I was responsible for Nick's death. But I really didn't know I was feeling that way. It's funny that I can look back now and understand what was making me tick, but I just couldn't

79

see it then. I didn't even know I had those sorts of feelings until I really thought about it. I still have a lot of bad days, but I'm feeling a lot better now.

FEELINGS ARE QUITE primitive. They are your first response to a situation, before you've had time to think. But having feelings—even bad ones—is not a bad thing; it's a necessary thing. You've no doubt been flooded with feelings since your loss, often without any conscious thought. If they're especially difficult to bear, you may well have wanted to be rid of them. But by now you know that no matter how much you write about your feelings, you still have them. *Expressing* feelings doesn't rid you of them but may help you to bear and manage them and even lighten the toll they are taking on you.

Becoming Aware of Feelings

Before you can consciously or intentionally express a feeling, you have to first realize that you're *having* one. And to prevent yourself from being swept away by a powerful feeling, you need to think about and understand it. Recognizing that you have a feeling is the "buffer," or bridge, betwen emotion and thought. Almost everything you do in this journal is a product of your thinking about your feelings and then expressing them. In this way, expression refers to venting and managing your emotions in a way that supports recovery.

But you don't have to think about and name a feeling to vent it. In fact, you don't even have to be consciously aware that you're having a feeling. Expressing a feeling without consciously thinking about it is called acting out. Acting out a feeling is not innately good or bad. There may be many times when it's importaant to behave spontaneously, without thinking about it. Crying

Expressing feelings doesn't rid you of them but may help you to bear and manage them and even lighten the toll they are taking on you.

Grief should be the instructor of the wise; Sorrow is Knowledge.
—LORD BYRON

is a good example of spontaneous behavior that is more often than not a great way to let off emotional energy. But feeling angry and yelling at someone is not a particularly positive way to let off steam, nor is overeating or drinking too much alcohol. These would be examples of acting out an emotion in a way that may be destructive to your relationships and yourself. In your grief work, you're trying to discover positive ways to express your feelings.

Since your loss you've been trying to manage and work toward overcoming unpleasant feelings. Critical to this goal is the ability to recognize and understand your feelings. This process of recognizing and thinking about your feelings is a step toward emotional *regulation*. Regulation doesn't mean stopping your feelings; rather, it allows you to find ways to express them positively instead of acting them out inappropriately. Simply put, coping with your feelings doesn't mean you don't have them. But it does mean you don't let them overwhelm you.

Something as simple as stopping and thinking about how you're feeling at a difficult moment can be a very useful way to regulate and cope with that emotion. The next journal entry will help you recognize how you're feeling, and why. It provides a checklist of very basic feelings, many of which you'll probably experience during your bereavement. This is a journal entry you should repeat often as you learn to focus on and process your emotions. Photocopy this entry format so you can use it repeatedly.

Complete this journal entry shortly before or after a situation that may be emotional for you in some way or another or when you find feelings washing over you. It's a simple way to help pick up on and understand a feeling.

Crying is a good example of spontaneous behavior that is more often than not a great way to let off emotional energy.

MY FEELINGS

How I Feel	Why I Feel This Way
_____ afraid	_____
_____ amused	_____
_____ angry	_____
_____ anxious	_____
_____ ashamed	_____
_____ bitter	_____
_____ detached	_____
_____ disappointed	_____
_____ foolish	_____
_____ guilty	_____
_____ happy	_____
_____ helpless	_____
_____ hopeful	_____
_____ hopeless	_____
_____ ignored	_____
_____ incapable	_____
_____ irritated	_____
_____ lonely	_____
_____ numb	_____
_____ overwhelmed	_____
_____ sad	_____
_____ trapped	_____
_____ vulnerable	_____
_____ worthless	_____
_____ yearning	_____

- Were you easily able to pick out feelings? If you've used this journal format more than once, is it getting easier to recognize your feelings?
- Do you understand why you feel the way you do? Is it important to understand how you feel?
- Do you want to be able to regulate your feelings? Does understanding your feelings help you to regulate them?

Thinking about Feelings

The entry you just completed is more a record of your feelings than an account of them. The entry helps you log your thoughts on why you were feeling a certain way, but stops there. It's very important to be able to recognize feelings if you're going to think about them—after all, your feelings usually lead to the way you behave. If you don't think before you act, you may later regret your actions.

The previous entry should be repeated many times so you can gauge and reflect on your feelings at a given moment. But to understand your feelings, you need to go beyond this. *Interoceptive* awareness is the ability to correctly recognize and interpret feelings as you have them. People with poor interoceptive awareness often misidentify their feelings. This is about knowing *how* you feel. On the other hand, *introspective* awareness is understanding *why* you feel the way you do.

Introspection consists of looking inside. Your journal is a record of that inward contemplation. Understanding your feelings doesn't expose you to the world, but it does expose you to *yourself*. Sometimes, people find it difficult to look at themselves in this way. But "knowing thyself" has always been a goal of education, and moving through the grieving process involves learning—about who you are.

By linking your feelings to your thoughts, you also link your

Interoceptive aware-ness is the ability to correctly recognize and interpret feelings as you have them. . . . This is about knowing how you feel.

feelings to your behaviors. You stop behaving impulsively or re-actively. You begin to see yourself more clearly and better understand why and how you respond to things, including your loss. Then you are in a better position to decide what to do next. The next journal entry is another that you should consider repeating. It will help you zero in on your feelings and begin to understand them. Before completing the entry, you may wish to photocopy it so that you may repeat it at a future time.

YOUR THOUGHTS ABOUT YOUR FEELINGS

1. List the feelings you checked off in the previous journal entry. If you picked more than six, just pick the six most powerful feelings you identified.

a. _____   d. _____

b. _____   e. _____

c. _____   f. _____

2. Of these feelings, which two were predominant?

a. _____

b. _____

THINGS TO THINK ABOUT

- Is it possible to have different feelings at the same time? How do you decide which is the predominant feeling?
- Is it possible to have feelings at the same time that contradict each other? How do you deal with the contradiction?

3. For this entry, pick one feeling to focus on: _____

a. Describe how you feel.

_____

_____

b. What situation led to this feeling?

_____

_____

_____

_____

c. Do you understand why you feel this way? If so, describe your reasons.

_____

_____

_____

_____

d. How did you handle the feeling?

_____

_____

_____

_____

4. Are you satisfied with the way you handled this feeling?

_____

_____

_____

_____

5. What changes might you make to better handle this feeling in the future?

_____

_____

_____

_____

THINGS TO THINK ABOUT

- Have you learned more about this feeling? Was your feeling more complicated than you initially thought it was?
- If you've used this journal format more than once, are you learning more about your feelings? What are you learning?
- Does understanding your feelings help you manage them?

Feelings and Moods

Moods are only problems when they frequently fluctuate from high to low or when the most common mood is a bad mood of some kind.

Some feelings last a while and are more like a collection of feelings rather than a single emotion. These are *moods*—a set of underlying feelings that color everything for you while in that mood. When people have feelings that change quickly or their feelings isolate them from others, they're often described as moody.

Clearly, there are good moods and bad ones—happy, angry, satisfied, depressed. Moods are only problems when they frequently fluctuate from high to low or when the most common mood is a bad mood of some kind. When moods are pervasive over time, they sometimes begin to interfere with your ability to function. At that point, a mood may be developing into a disorder that needs treatment. For instance, if you're often depressed, or you're depressed all the time, you'll find that *everything* is affected by your mood: your sleep, your appetite, your energy, your ability to concentrate. The same is true if you're anxious all the time, or angry. Moods can become so deep that they change the way you see and feel about everything.

As you move through your grief work, you'll no doubt experience many moods. Most of these you will overcome, but some may seem insurmountable. If that becomes your experience, it will be important to think about some of the things you've already considered in this journal—how and where to get support and what and when to share with your community.

The most useful time to write about a feeling is when you're having it. Similarly, the most useful time to think about a mood is when you're in it. *Complete the next journal entry only when you're in the grip of a mood.* Look over the entry now, but skip it and return only when you can write about a mood when you're actually experiencing it. You may not *want* to write when in an emotionally difficult mood, but this is the challenge and discipline of writing. If you want to use your journal for your recovery, you need to explore your feelings while you're feeling them.

If you repeat the entry each time you're caught in the same mood, or in another mood, you'll learn a great deal about yourself. Like most of the journal entries in *The Healing Journey Through Grief*, the entries in this chapter are worth repeating at least several times. Thinking and writing about your feelings once is only a start to understanding and learning how to cope with them. Of course, not all moods are bad. Some are light-hearted and fun, and these moods are important to write about too. As you move through your grief work, you'll experience more and more good moods. Don't limit your entries to only unpleasant or bad moods—remember to think about your positive moods also.

HOW DO YOU FEEL RIGHT NOW?

1. What kind of mood are you in?

_____

_____

_____

_____

_____

2. Describe your mood in a single word: _____

3. What are the main emotions in this mood?

_____

_____

_____

4. Put your mood into words.

a. *This mood is . . .* _____

b. *If this mood had a color, it would be . . .* _____

c. *If this mood had texture, it would be . . .* _____

d. *If this mood made a noise, it would sound like . . .* _____

5. Describe your mood in more depth.

I feel . . . _____

_____

_____

_____

_____

6. What brought this mood on?

_____

_____

_____

7. How long have you been feeling this way?

_____

_____

8. Is this a common mood for you? If it is, describe it.

_____

_____

_____

9. Is this mood so strong that it's interfering with your daily life? If so, briefly describe how. _____

_____

THINGS TO THINK ABOUT

- If this is an unpleasant mood, what can you do to avoid situations that contribute to this mood? If it is a pleasant mood, what sort of situations or relationships stimulate this mood and keep it alive?
- If you've completed this entry more than once, do you have a clearer sense of your moods and what affects them?
- Have the types or frequency of your moods changed over time since your loss? In what ways?
- Are your moods so long lasting or intense that they affect your ability to function? If they are, do you feel you need help with them?

The Predictability of Feelings

As you may have discovered through the last journal entry, there are some situations that are going to arouse certain kinds of feelings in you. Sometimes the feelings are unpleasant. Other times a certain situation may evoke a warm feeling or memory.

When feelings can be tied to certain kinds of situations, you can do something about them. Knowing that being around family makes you feel safe and comfortable tells you that this is a good place to be—when you're feeling anxious, turning to your family can help. On the other hand, if you know that passing a certain landmark every day on your way to work brings back sad and depressing memories, you can change your route to work. Knowing your "triggers" allows you to take more control over your life.

Triggers are those things in your life that activate or arouse feelings and reactions. They can be people, sounds, smells, or situations—anything, in fact, that brings back memories or feelings. As people usually want to enjoy pleasant thoughts and feelings, it's only the things that trigger unpleasant memories and emotions that are to be avoided. Triggers that stimulate good feelings and nostalgia should be embraced. Understanding your triggers can help you decide what to move toward and what to move away from on your healing journey.

Understanding your triggers can help you decide what to move toward and what to move away from on your healing journey.

All this is a way of saying that many of your feelings are predictable. You can almost count on them under certain conditions—and this allows you to do something about them. If you know it's going to rain, although you can't stop the rain you can wear a raincoat.

The next entry is designed to help you look at those things that trigger unpleasant or distressing feelings themselves. You can easily adapt it to write about positive triggers as well—and there are several other entries later in *The Healing Journey Through Grief* that will help you express pleasant memories, remembrances, and nostalgia.

TRIGGERS

1. Are there certain types of situations that trigger feelings in you? Describe them.

_____

_____

_____

_____

2. Are there certain people who are triggers for you? Who are they?

_____

_____

_____

_____

3. Are there things besides situations and people that are triggers for you—sights, smells, or sounds or music, movies, or clothing?

_____

_____

_____

_____

4. What emotions or thoughts do these things trigger?

_____

_____

_____

_____

_____

_____

5. Why do these things trigger these feelings and thoughts?

_____

_____

_____

_____

6. If these are the sorts of feelings you want to avoid, what can you do to avoid the triggers? What alternatives are there?

_____

_____

_____

_____

_____

Displacing Your Feelings

Displacing your feelings onto others — "dumping" — is not fair to them, and it keeps you from dealing directly with the real source of your feelings.

After a bad day at work, you might feel annoyed at the first pedestrian who doesn't cross the road fast enough. Or you might find yourself getting easily irritated at something you hear on the news. You may go home and yell at the kids — even though you realize it's not really the kids you're mad at. On the other hand, when things are going well, you may find that everything looks good. These are examples of displaced feelings — feelings about one thing that get placed on another.

At this time in your life — when you're experiencing many difficult moments, feelings, and moods — it's easy to displace your feelings onto someone or something else. Displacement most easily occurs when you're not conscious of doing it. It begins when you're not even aware you're having a feeling or when you're trying to squash the feeling and pretend it's not there. But not recognizing the feeling or choosing to ignore it doesn't make it go away. Instead, the feeling gets expressed — sometimes in very negative ways — through displacement. You may let off steam in the wrong way and probably at the wrong person.

It would be better to express your fears, anger, and disappointment directly. Displacing your feelings onto others — "dumping" — is not fair to them, and it keeps you from dealing directly with the real source of your feelings.

As you complete the work in this chapter, it's important for you to be in touch with your feelings and how you express them. Feelings are like weather vanes in that they don't explain the weather, but they directly show you the direction and intensity of the wind. Feelings are the weather vane to your emotions—they don't necessarily offer insight into *why* you might be feeling emotional, but they are the direct line "inside." If you stay in touch with your feelings, you'll have an important gauge to your emotional health that can help you control your emotions rather than let your emotions control you.

WATCHING YOUR FEELINGS

It's not always easy to put a name on feelings. Emotions are often too complex. You may find that you've experienced feelings that have no simple name or that are composites of several feelings. "Confused," for instance, is really not a feeling, but more a mixture of feelings or an inability to name a single feeling.

1. Give names to six other feelings (or mixes of feelings) that you've had which have not been otherwise named in this chapter:

a. _____   d. _____

b. _____   e. _____

c. _____   f. _____

2. During your bereavement, you're experiencing a lot of feelings that are negative and can interfere with your functioning. Are there feelings that you can *use* to help in your recovery and general sense of well-being?

_____

_____

_____

_____

_____

3. Do you displace your feelings? Onto whom or what?

_____

_____

_____

_____

_____

4. Do you need to find healthier or more appropriate ways to express your feelings?

_____

_____

_____

_____

_____

THINGS TO THINK ABOUT

- What have you learned about the way you deal with feelings?
- Will you be repeating these journal entries in order to delve into and understand your feelings in more detail? Are there entry formats that you find particularly helpful? Why?
- Do you think that understanding your feelings will help you deal with your grief? In what ways?
- Do you think understanding your feelings will help you deal better with other people in your life? Who, and why?

Checking in with Your Road Map: Stage 2

By now you've entered, or are near, the second stage in your grief work—Emotional Immersion and Deconstruction. During this stage, you're moving from an acceptance and realization of the death to catharsis, a point where you can vent and let go of your feelings. During this part of your journey, you'll often be faced with intense feelings, and you'll ask many questions, often

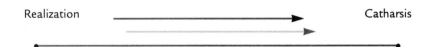

Realization ———————————————▶ Catharsis

Stage 2: Emotional Immersion and Deconstruction

of a spiritual, philosophical, or religious nature, trying to make sense of things. Your world deconstructs as a result of your loss, but by the end of this stage, you'll have built the foundation on which you're going to reconstruct your life. During this stage, you'll experience intense feelings that linger and then leave, only to return again. You'll also think deeply about your loss and the world in which you've been left. As you near and then enter this second stage in your grief work, the initial goals are not only to feel your emotions but also to begin to understand and vent them in ways that help, not hinder, your journey.

"Winter is come and gone, But grief returns with the revolving year."
—PERCY BYSSHE SHELLEY

CHECKPOINT: STAGES

Circle the letter that most closely describes where you are *right now* with each task.

Stage 1 Tasks	I'm not ready to deal with this task.	I'm working on this task.	I've completed this task.
Adjusting	A	B	C
Functioning	A	B	C
Keeping in check	A	B	C
Accepting support	A	B	C
Stage 2 Tasks			
Contending with reality	A	B	C
Development of insight	A	B	C
Reconstructing personal values and beliefs	A	B	C
Acceptance and letting go	A	B	C

Stage 3 Tasks	I'm not ready to deal with this task.	I'm working on this task.	I've completed this task.
Development of social relations	A	B	C
Decisions about changes in lifestyle	A	B	C
Renewal of self-awareness	A	B	C
Acceptance of responsibility	A	B	C

THINGS TO THINK ABOUT

- Are you more in Stage 1 or Stage 2 of your grief at this time? Are you ready to deal with Stage 2 issues at this point along your journey, or do you need to do more work on the tasks of Stage 1?

- Are you emotionally ready for the tasks involved in finding acceptance and meaning? Do you need to talk to someone about what you're going through, or do you need help or support to tackle and deal with these tasks?

8

Destination:
COPING WITH FEELINGS

*"When sorrows come,
they come not
single spies, But in
battalions!"*
—WILLIAM
SHAKESPEARE

ELAINE

*My father died when I was twelve. I actually can't remember very
much about his death other than it was a weird time. No one in my
immediate family—my mother, older brother, or two older sisters
—was able to deal with the death well, and that's what really affected me the most.*

*My dad died unexpectedly, during a quick hospitalization. I didn't
even know he was in the hospital until I came home from school and
a neighbor told me. I figured out he had died later that night when
I was in my bedroom, because I overheard all the noise from down-
stairs, while my mother and sisters were crying. It was one of my sisters who actually told me about the death the next morning, but
even then the details were vague. I didn't get to go the funeral, and
no one in the family ever really dealt directly with our loss.*

*Over the next few years, when I was a teenager, my family came
unglued. My mom began to drink heavily, and I often found her outside the house sitting on the curb, drunk and crying. My sisters got
into more and more arguments with Mom and with each other. My
brother just got more and more into his own life, and more removed*

97

from the rest of us. He was six years older than me and joined the army within two years and was gone. I haven't had much contact with him since. Things got worse at home, with lots of arguments, and my oldest sister basically got thrown out by Mom when she was sixteen and began living with a friend's family. My mom never dealt with her alcoholism and became more and more physically frail. By the time she remarried, she was really a wreck. The second marriage failed quickly, and my mom died of cancer within a year, when I was seventeen. They told us that her insides were just riddled with the disease and that her liver or heart would have killed her if her cancer hadn't. I still see my sisters, but not until recently have we talked about the past, and we've still never really talked about the death of both our parents. We just weren't a family that could cope.

YOU FACE MANY sorrows in your mourning. They may be the first thing you feel at the beginning of your day or the last thing at night. Your emotions are usually the first thing you experience. Reflections, thoughts, and behavior follow.

There are many ways to describe coping—to contend with; to endure, to manage, to survive; to struggle with. But in the final analysis, to cope means to deal with a situation. As you work through your grief, you'll face many things with which you'll have to contend, but most of all you'll have to find ways to cope with your own feelings.

Coping with your feelings in healthy ways helps; trying to cope in unhealthy ways invariably does not. The painful feeling or problem situation still remains, and chances are you're worse off than when you began.

Healthy and Unhealthy Coping

Emotions are the things you *feel*. Your behaviors are the things you *do*. Your feelings affect your behaviors and sometimes shape them. Coping is what you do to handle your feelings so that they don't overwhelm you. Healthy coping means finding ways to effectively expose what you are feeling. When you act out your feelings in ways that are self-destructive or self-defeating—such as not taking care of yourself, leaving responsibilities unfulfilled, or turning to addictive substances—you're demonstrating inadequate coping skills.

Self-destructive and self-defeating behaviors are those that get in the way of and interfere with your broader goals. In an effort to get rid of a bad feeling, instead of trying to work through and manage it, you may do things that are counterproductive. For instance, the use of alcohol or drugs to drown out or numb a feeling is an example of a self-destructive behavior. It not only doesn't resolve the situation that's upsetting you, but can also create all sorts of other problems for you. Yelling needlessly at someone on whom you count for support and help is an example of behavior that is self-defeating. You may succeed only in pushing that person away and damaging the relationship, thus reducing the very support you need.

However, there are also many examples of healthy coping—from journal writing to physical exercise to meditation. Some people talk through their feelings. Others use art and music as a way to "soothe the savage soul." Still others may seek company and be among other people.

When you act out your feelings in ways that are self-destructive or self-defeating—such as not taking care of yourself, leaving responsibilities unfulfilled, or turning to addictive substances—you're demonstrating inadequate coping skills.

HOW DO YOU COPE?

1. What are the most pressing things you have to cope with?

_____

_____

_____

_____

2. What are the greatest obstacles to overcoming these things?

_____

_____

_____

_____

3. In what healthy ways do you cope? Check off all that apply, and add your own.

_____ art   _____ dance   _____ exercise

_____ gardening   _____ hobbies   _____ listening to music

_____ meditation   _____ movies   _____ playing an instrument

_____ reading   _____ sports   _____ talking

_____ therapy   _____ walking   _____ writing

other: _____   _____

_____   _____

_____   _____

_____   _____

_____   _____

4. Do you ever behave self-destructively? Give examples.

_____

_____

_____

_____

5. In what ways is your behavior self-defeating?

_____

_____

_____

_____

6. What is your healthiest coping mechanism?

_____

_____

7. What is your unhealthiest coping mechanism?

_____

_____

THINGS TO THINK ABOUT

- What most prevents you from coping with a feeling or situation? What most helps?
- Do you keep hidden from others any of your unhealthy coping mechanisms? If so, why?

Becoming Aware of Your Behaviors

You don't have to be consciously aware of your feelings or thoughts in order to behave. In fact, what we most often call behavior is simply a reaction to things, which involves little intentional thought. You usually don't think about and consider every aspect of your behavior — you just react to the situation. Most of the time, that's fine. But sometimes it's important to think about your behavior *before* you behave and to reflect on what motivates your behavior. These are the times when your behavior may be the wrong response, such as when what you do gets you into trouble or takes you further from your goals. It's not important to consider everything you do before you do it (that would be a strange way to live), but it is important to know how you feel and why you act the way you do. Balancing spontaneity and consideration leads to the development of decision-making skills. When people are spontaneous but not reflective, they're impulsive. When people endlessly consider without acting, they're indecisive or timid. As with many things, the trick is in the balancing.

WHAT YOU DO IS WHO YOU ARE

1. Do you ever behave in ways you later regret? Describe them.

_____

_____

_____

_____

_____

_____

2. Do you ever _not_ behave in ways you later wish you had? Describe them.

_____

_____

_____

_____

_____

_____

3. Check off only those words that best describe your most frequent behaviors since your loss. Feel free to add other words that describe your actions.

_____ aggressive	_____ angry	_____ caring	_____ confused
_____ considerate	_____ courageous	_____ depressed	_____ disagreeable
_____ distant	_____ fearful	_____ flexible	_____ friendly
_____ insecure	_____ manipulative	_____ obsessive	_____ outgoing
_____ rigid	_____ sad	_____ selfish	_____ withdrawn

other: _____   _____

_____   _____

_____   _____

_____   _____

4. Has your behavior changed since your loss? In what ways?

_____

_____

_____

_____

_____

5. What behaviors do you often use? Check off all that apply, and add your own.

_____ yelling   _____ laughing   _____ drinking

_____ withdrawing   _____ walking   _____ smoking

_____ drug use   _____ interacting with others   _____ talking

other: _____   _____   _____

_____   _____   _____

_____   _____   _____

_____   _____   _____

_____   _____   _____

6. In reflection, are these the sort of behaviors you want to use and be seen using?

_____

_____

_____

7. What message are you giving other people through your behavior? Do you mean to give this message? If you do, why?

_____

_____

_____

_____

_____

8. If your behavior has changed, *why* has it?

_____

_____

_____

_____

9. Is there more to you than your behavior? What would you like people to know about you that they can't tell by your behavior?

_____

_____

_____

_____

10. Are there changes you want to make in your behavior? Name them.

_____

_____

_____

THINGS TO THINK ABOUT

- People often judge you by your "outside" person—through your behavior. Is there a different "inside" person?
- Do you feel okay about your behavior? Are there changes you want—or need—to make?
- Do you feel okay about the way that people see you? Do you wish they could see something different? What would that be?

Understanding and Coping

Understanding your behavior is one aspect of coping. But in the case of your bereavement, coping also means finding ways to live with your feelings, unbearable and overwhelming as they may be at times. Coping is the process that keeps you on track as you move through your grief work and allows you to not get derailed along the way. To cope with your feelings, you really don't have to understand them. But understanding your feelings *helps* you to cope, because it helps you to recognize what's affecting you; and that allows you to make *informed* choices about how best to deal with things. Feelings are important—they help tell us what's going on. Like physical pain, negative emotions are important also. Ridding or numbing yourself to feelings is like taking a medication to mask pain.

Unhealthy coping behaviors may help to block the feelings in the short run—that's their appeal—but they don't address the problem, and they certainly don't cure it. The real aim of coping is to *tolerate* and *manage* the feelings so that you can achieve the long-term goal of dealing with and overcoming the situations causing the pain in the first place. Healthy coping entails:

Understanding your feelings helps you to cope, because it helps you to recognize what's affecting you; and that allows you to make informed choices about how best to deal with things.

- knowing when you have feelings—being in touch with what's going on inside

- identifying your feelings—recognizing and being able to name the feelings

- tolerating your feelings—accepting the feelings, and not trying to escape them

- managing your feelings—controlling your feelings, not letting them control you

- understanding your feelings—connecting your feelings to their causes

By now, you've spent time thinking about your feelings in general and about your coping style. Using the next journal entry, concentrate on only one feeling that requires coping skills. You can pick any of the feelings you named in earlier journal entries, or use this entry to write about a specific feeling you may be having at any given moment.

ONE AT A TIME

Use this entry to express one feeling at a time. Repeat the entry to revisit the same feeling again, or use it to think about a different feeling. This is a free-form entry; write whatever comes into your mind.

The feeling for this entry: _____

1. Describe this feeling.

_____

_____

_____

_____

_____

2. How does this feeling affect your behavior?

_____

_____

_____

_____

_____

3. How do you usually deal with this feeling?

_____

_____

_____

_____

4. Are you able to successfully cope with this feeling? Why or why not?

_____

_____

_____

5. How will you deal with this feeling in the long run?

_____

_____

_____

_____

THINGS TO THINK ABOUT

- Do you deal with this feeling well? Does it ever get the better of you?
- What will happen in the long run if you don't learn to cope with this feeling?
- Are there many feelings that are difficult for you to deal with or just one or two?
- In general, what helps the most in dealing with difficult feelings?

Developing Coping Mechanisms That Work

In the end, coping really means using those helping behaviors that actually help—the things that you do that make you feel better. There's no such thing as a negative coping strategy, although there are negative behaviors that are ineffective *attempts* to cope. Few people would seriously suggest that not leaving your house or getting drunk every night in order to deal with grief are coping behaviors you should adopt. These may help temporarily deaden the pain, but they postpone the inevitable and don't help recovery. In fact, they delay it. We may make attempts to cope in all sorts of ways—positive and negative—

but, by definition, coping involves only the positive and healthy behaviors.

By now, you probably have a good idea of what you can do to help yourself deal with your feelings and an equally clear idea of what you shouldn't do—or at least what you should avoid.

But one of the lures of the negative behaviors is that they are "instant" tension relievers, even if they don't work in the long run. To many, it feels relaxing to have a few drinks and even better to get drunk and forget their sorrows, at least for a while. They may feel the same is true for other drugs too—feeling high makes them quickly forget their worries. For some people, it feels good to yell at someone or kick the dog in order to let off steam. Most of the negative behaviors provide instant relief, which makes them attractive. But they have big costs attached—sometimes for you *and* someone else (like the person you yelled at) and sometimes just for you.

It's pretty easy to *say* what's good for you and *name* what helps and what should be avoided. It's really hard, though, to actually *do* the things that are good for you and give up or avoid those things that aren't. It's not only hard to actually give up something that provides quick relief, but it's perhaps even more difficult to take on different behaviors. For instance, if you're not an outgoing person to begin with, it can be a big challenge to begin to connect with people for support.

One great value of a personal journal is that it allows you the chance to think about all these issues, experiment with your thinking, and express your thoughts and feelings *in private*. A journal requires nothing of you, except honesty. If you continue to use your journal honestly, you'll be able to see more clearly which way you want to go and be better able to make informed personal decisions about your grief and how to best handle and work through it.

CHECKPOINT: COPING

1. What have you learned about your coping behaviors?

_____

_____

_____

_____

_____

2. How do your coping behaviors work, and *why* do they work?

_____

_____

_____

_____

3. Which coping methods do you most typically choose?

_____

_____

_____

4. Are your coping behaviors positive or negative?

_____

_____

_____

5. How well are you coping?

_____

_____

_____

_____

6. In what ways would you like to improve your coping skills?

_____

_____

_____

_____

THINGS TO THINK ABOUT

- Is your journal helping you work your way through your grief? How honest are you being in your journal?
- Are you having special difficulties coping or changing your coping behaviors? Do you need help, from either friends or a professional therapist?
- How would you know if your coping methods were negative? Could you ask friends?

9

Destination:

FINDING MEANING

"To everything there is a season, and a time to every purpose under the heaven; a time to be born and time to die."

—ECCLESIASTES 3:1—8

ED

My life completely dropped out from under me when my son died. He was only eight, and full of life. One day he was here, and then gone.

I can't understand why this happened. Why, in a world with so many people who've lived a full life, should life be robbed from one so young? Where's the fairness in an innocent like Tim dying when there are people who probably don't deserve to live in the first place? At first, I tried to tell myself that Timmy had gone to a better place, that there was some order—some higher meaning—to all this, which I just couldn't understand. But I can't buy that. There's just nothing right about this, and I'm not going to pretend that it's okay he died. If this is the kind of god we have, then I don't want any part of him or his religion.

Since Tim's death, I've lost faith in just about everything. Nothing is right. I can't find meaning in anything anymore. I feel like I've got nothing left to live for, and every day is just another pointless day in a meaningless world, where you can't depend on anything.

MEANING IS THAT thing in our lives that adds richness and depth. Meaning gives significance and often provides purpose and direction. Without meaning, life can be empty. A birthday is just another day, unless you give it special meaning. If you're retired, every day can be just like the last or every day like a holiday—it all depends on the meaning you give to it. The glass can be half empty or half full.

Once you've lost someone close, things never return to the way they were before. And you will never again be the person you were before. The personal changes may be subtle, or they may be enormous. For some, the changes may be so subtle that no one even notices them. But hopefully, through keeping this journal, even the slight changes will be apparent to you, because the meaning you impart to those changes is critically important to your healing journey.

Deconstruction

Death takes away many things. It robs you of your loved one and sometimes your hopes and beliefs as well. It may be that your loved one was too young to die, or your life together was just beginning. Perhaps the death is unfair on the children who remain behind. Or your loved one may have experienced pain that seemed needless and unfair. There are many scenarios, all of which can leave the survivors confused and unable to understand how or why this could have happened. Often, the bereaved seek to find meaning for a death that seems to have none. A death that seems unfair or senseless can seriously challenge the philosophical, spiritual, or religious beliefs of even the most devout believers and leave them with a sense of meaninglessness.

The loss of an important person in your life can lead to a sense of "deconstruction"—the removal of the things that underpin

A death that seems unfair or senseless can seriously challenge the philosophical, spiritual, or religious beliefs of even the most devout believers and leave them with a sense of meaninglessness.

and make up your life. Some of these things may be practical, such as shared parenting, finances, or companionship. Others are the relational ties into which you may have poured your emotions and pinned your aspirations. All these things can make you feel like your life is falling to pieces, as if there is no longer anything to which you can attach your practical or emotional plans. At this time, although you may be past the initial shock of the death, you are quite likely experiencing the full depths of your emotions. In this state, the sense of deconstruction can heighten your sense of loss and despair even further.

It's easy to get stuck in any stage of the grief process and to move no further emotionally. In such a case, although you will inevitably move on with your life, you won't have found the resolution and peace that completed grief work can provide. If you get stuck in the stage where meaning is deconstructed, you may have great difficulty believing in anything again, trusting in the permanence of relationships, or building a new life for yourself.

Even though you've been introduced to grief work as something that moves through a progression of stages, the fact is that the process of grief work is not that linear. As you have no doubt discovered for yourself, you don't move through each aspect of your bereavement, check it off, and then move on. The earliest stages of your grief work deal with a basic adjustment and acclimation. They simply set the stage for your later grief work, in which the goals are not only a more meaningful acceptance of your loss but also a sense of being at peace with it.

The goal then, at this point in your grief work, is to explore and understand the way in which your beliefs and faith may have been shaken so that you can build a platform upon which to *re*construct and restore beliefs and meaning.

The goal is to explore and understand the way in which your beliefs and faith may have been shaken so that you can build a platform upon which to reconstruct and restore beliefs and meaning.

"Grief drives men into habits of serious reflection, sharpens the understanding and softens the heart."
—JOHN ADAMS

THE QUALITY OF LIFE

You've experienced the death of someone important in your life. In previous journal entries, you've thought and written about how that loss has affected you and your life. In many ways, those entries focused on emotional and practical changes—the concrete experiences of death. For this set of entries, which deal with meaning, you need to think about how your loss has changed the way you feel about life. First take a few moments to think about how your life has changed since the death.

1. What has your life been like since the passing of your loved one?

_____

_____

_____

_____

2. What are the three most difficult things to accept about the death?

a. _____

b. _____

c. _____

3. What three changes has it been the most difficult to adjust to?

a. _____

b. _____

c. _____

4. Your loved one has been lost to you. What else has been lost from your life? (Here, think about the *quality* of your life.)

_____

_____

_____

_____

5. Has something changed in how you see or feel about the world since the death? How would you describe this change?

_____

_____

> **THINGS TO THINK ABOUT**
>
> - Does the world seem like a different place? Have your beliefs about the world been questioned in some way by this loss?
> - Do you feel as though your world has lost some meaning? If so, is this is a serious challenge to your sense of meaning and order in the world, or does it simply require some time to adjust?

The Meaning of Meaning

Faith, meaning, beliefs, purpose—these are all words that are used to describe similar things. In the end, they boil down to the same thing: they provide us with a way to make sense of the world, especially those things that are so hard to logically or clearly understand. When we give meaning to something, we invest in it a special power—the power for that thing to be accepted as part of life. Death is but one example of events we accept but don't necessarily understand.

Our beliefs embody the things we presume to be true. They include our ideas of how things are or should be, and our lives and actions hinge on these beliefs. Meaning provides the substance on which beliefs are built. Together, belief and meaning offer the following.

- *Direction*. This provides a basis for decision making about what to do with your life, how to behave, and sometimes ideals about what's right and what's wrong.

- *Principles*. They produce fundamental ideas on which to base your behavior, decisions, and relationships.

"It is our human lot, it is heaven's will, that sorrow follow joy."
—TITUS MACCIUS PLAUTUS

- *Purpose.* Establishing a purpose makes your life goal oriented and provides you with some final goal toward which you can move.

- *Reason.* Reason offers a justification and underlying logic to your world and provides motivation for the things you do.

- *Significance.* This gives a "texture" to life, a quality that adds value and consequence to the things you do and the things that occur within your life.

Although beliefs and meaning are sometimes based on actual experiences, they're usually *subjective* experiences. More often than not, beliefs and meaning are usually things you feel, but they cannot be "proved" to be true. They are often a state of mind.

Faith is that part of a belief system that allows you to believe without having to prove the basis for your beliefs. It allows you to find meaning without having to demonstrate the correctness of that meaning. There are many versions of faith: a belief in God or another divine being, faith in a situation, belief in friends. You may have faith that your decisions are the right decisions, or you may have faith that things in the world are the way they are for a reason, even if you don't understand them. With faith, you take for granted the truth of belief and meaning.

MEANING IN YOUR LIFE

1. Check all that apply. Do you think of yourself as:

_____ philosophical   _____ religious   _____ spiritual

Other: _____

2. Briefly describe your answer to the preceding question.

I believe . . . _____

_____

_____

3. What sort of underlying philosophy or belief system helps guide you or shape your behaviors?

_____

_____

_____

_____

_____

4. Do you consider yourself to be someone of faith? What does faith mean to you?

_____

_____

_____

_____

_____

5. How has your loss affected your faith or the meaning you give to the world?

_____

_____

_____

_____

_____

THINGS TO THINK ABOUT

- Do you normally think about your beliefs, or do they simply remain in the background of your life? Have you found yourself thinking more about your belief system since your loss?
- Have your beliefs helped you to understand and accept your loss, or has your loss shaken your sense of faith or your beliefs?

Finding Meaning

Beliefs and meaning give comfort and allow the world to remain an orderly place, even during the emotional chaos following a death.

Beliefs and meaning give comfort and allow the world to remain an orderly place, even during the emotional chaos following a death. If you already have a strong belief system, you may be able to give meaning to your loss through your beliefs. You may believe that the death has some meaning, even if it's not clear to you. For example, it isn't unusual for those with strong religious beliefs to speak about a "greater purpose" or of the deceased going to a "better place." These are examples of people finding or giving meaning to something that might otherwise be overwhelming if devoid of any meaning at all.

People actively seek meaning in their lives. Meaning helps the bereaved to accept their loss and move on; it helps make the death seem more acceptable. For instance, where there's social injustice involved, you may hear the bereaved say that the death has value if it serves to bring about a social change or a new attitude in others. When someone has died through the negligence or the intent of someone else—a drunk driver or a drive-by shooter, perhaps—the bereaved seek justice. Here the bereaved speak of giving the death meaning through the process of getting legal justice. Sometimes those who have died needlessly through the hands of another or an unjust society are memorialized in name through the changes their death has brought—as in the case of Megan's Law, for instance.

The effort to make the loss stand for something is one way that people seek to find or recover meaning from an otherwise meaningless situation. Bereaved parents who build an organization to help others avoid a similar loss, or assist those who have experienced the same loss, are not only lending help to others but also memorializing their own loss and giving *personal* meaning to the death. Others may seek a different kind of meaning—a personal

"Although we know that after such a loss the acute stage of mourning will subside, we also know we shall remain inconsolable and will never find a substitute. No matter what may fill the gap . . . it nevertheless remains something else. And actually, this is how it should be; it is the only way of perpetuating that love which we do not want to relinquish."

—SIGMUND FREUD

meaning that is more spiritual and inward rather than directed outward to society as a whole.

If you have a strong set of guiding beliefs, you'll have a sense of where to turn to find meaning. For others, finding meaning may involve searching through your life and intense self-examination. In either case, finding meaning may be difficult, but the first step is knowing *where* to look. The second is knowing *how* to look.

Finding meaning may be difficult, but the first step is knowing where to look. The second is knowing how to look.

THE INGREDIENTS OF MEANING

1. In what ways was your loved one an ingredient in your life that added depth and meaning?

_____

_____

_____

_____

2. Can you find guidance or meaning in your current beliefs?

_____

_____

_____

_____

3. Look around you. What other ingredients in your life continue to give you direction and meaning and serve to shape and define your life? Check off all that apply, and add at least three other elements of your life that provide meaning.

_____ career   _____ children   _____ community involvement

_____ friends   _____ hobbies   _____ pets

_____ parents   _____ religion   _____ spouse

other: _____   _____

_____   _____

_____   _____

4. In what ways do these things hold meaning for you?

_____

_____

_____

_____

_____

5. What other things in your life contribute to its richness and depth?

_____

_____

_____

_____

6. What meaning resides in the tasks of your daily life or in the special tasks that you may have taken on since the death?

_____

_____

_____

_____

_____

The last question in this entry is free form. Look back at what you've just written and think about it for a moment. Then complete the following sentence, without stopping. Follow your thoughts wherever they take you, without lifting your pen from the page.

7. *I derive meaning in my life . . .* _____

_____

_____

_____

Meaning and Personal Growth

Once shaken, meaning can be completely lost. The loss of meaning can create intense emotional difficulty for the bereaved. It may be that since the death of your child or spouse, you see no purpose to your own life. So the struggle you face is to reconstruct meaning for yourself.

It's true that meaning can be lost, but it can also be renewed or transformed completely following a death. In fact, people often discover meaning after loss where they may not have had any before. There are many instances of people finding spirituality for the first time or, following a dramatic change, developing an entirely new set of principles on which to build their lives. Tragedy can trigger strength and growth.

Beliefs are not limited to the religious or spiritual. Whatever the nature of your beliefs, they can help you to understand and accept your loss and provide a way to put it into perspective. Beliefs can help you to accept and move on, not without regrets and sadness but with hope and courage to face the future. Beyond this, finding personal meaning suggests that the death can actually provide insights into life and help you not only to accept the loss but in some way also to experience personal growth through it.

No one seeks personal growth through the loss of someone dear to them. But it is possible to draw inspiration and learn from the death, once the reality of it has sunk in.

Beliefs can help you to accept and move on, not without regrets and sadness but with hope and courage to face the future.

PERSONAL MEANING

1. How can memories of your loved one provide support as you seek meaning?

_____

_____

_____

_____

2. What would your loved one want for you at this time in your life? What advice or direction would she or he offer you at this time?

_____

_____

_____

_____

_____

3. Are there any special lessons or meanings that you can draw from the death of your loved one?

_____

_____

_____

_____

_____

4. What have you learned about life through this death?

_____

_____

_____

_____

_____

5. What has your loss taught you about relationships?

_____

_____

_____

_____

_____

6. What is the most important thing you've learned through your loss?

_____

_____

_____

_____

_____

7. How has loss added meaning to your life? How have you grown as a person?

_____

_____

_____

_____

THINGS TO THINK ABOUT

- Has this loss helped you to personally grow in some way? If it has, were you surprised to realize you've grown? If it hasn't, what do you think is holding back your ability to help yourself find personal meaning?
- What's it like to realize that you can grow, even through loss?

Making Meaning

Finding meaning is no substitute for your loss, but it will help to sustain you and provide the substance from which you can rebuild your life.

As you probably already know, meaning doesn't necessarily come easy. No matter how hard you search for meaning, you may still find life itself or some aspect of it empty. And no matter how much meaning you find, it won't erase your emotions or explain away the death.

But the point is not to erase your loss—it's to begin and continue the process of reconstructing meaning in your life. For many, meaning isn't something that simply exists—it's something to be discovered or created. As you move forward along your healing journey, you'll learn how to discover meaning in the "found" materials of your life—in your memories, your relationships, and your environment. Finding meaning is no substitute for your loss, but it will help to sustain you and provide the substance from which you can rebuild your life after death.

FRAGMENTS OF MEANING

This and the following journal entry offer a different way to explore and discover meaning. For this entry, you'll create a collage—a compilation of photographs and parts of photographs, words, and other materials that are arranged and pasted to create a new picture. Go through your collection of photographs, magazines, and books, and cut out entire or parts of photos and pictures as well as words. Use only those pictures and words that remind you in some way of your loved one or your loss. *As you select and cut out your materials, don't think about the finished collage—pick each item based only on how that particular thing attracts or affects you.* Once you've cut out and collected each piece you want to use, paste them together in the space provided in this book or on a separate sheet of paper if you prefer. If you use the space provided here, you'll obviously have to be conscious of size. Once you've completed the collage, take some time to look carefully at it and think about how it makes you feel. Then complete the entry by answering the questions that follow the collage space.

CREATE YOUR COLLAGE IN THIS SPACE

1. Look back at the collage you've just created. How does it make you feel?

_____

_____

_____

_____

_____

2. What does your collage mean? Can you find words to describe its meaning?

_____

_____

_____

_____

_____

_____

THINGS TO THINK ABOUT

- What was it like to simply create without words? Did the process of collage making succeed in expressing feelings?
- Were you able to find meaning in the process of making the collage? Were you able to find meaning in the finished collage?
- Is collage making something you want to do again? Are there other forms of artwork that might help you express feelings and explore meaning?

A FRIDGE POEM

It's possible to make meaning out of a jumble of bits and pieces. In completing your collage, you did just that. As you take disconnected parts and connect them, you *create* meaning through the process of connection. But it's only after you've built the connective links and created something new that you're able to look for the meaning within.

In this entry, you're going to create a "fridge poem." The entry is named for the magnetic refrigerator poetry kits that have recently become popular. These kits are made up of hundreds of individual words that are magnetized, and by arranging them in the desired order you can create messages or poems on your refrigerator.

For this entry, you can buy a fridge poetry kit or simply cut out one hundred words *at random* from any magazine. Then select from among them between thirty-five and fifty words. From these, create a poem inspired by your loss.

1. Once you've completed the poem, reproduce it here.

_____

_____

_____

_____

_____

_____

_____

_____

_____

_____

2. Reread your poem. How does rereading it make you feel?

_____

_____

_____

_____

_____

3. What meaning is there in this poem for you?

_____

_____

_____

_____

_____

_____

_____

THINGS TO THINK ABOUT

- What's the difference between *making* meaning and *finding* meaning? Did you make meaning from, or find it within, the words you chose for your poem?
- Do you have to look for meaning to find it? How can you keep finding meaning?

10

Destination:
REFLECTING

"There is something pleasurable in calm remembrance of a past sorrow."
——MARCUS TULLIUS CICERO

RUTH

After Paul died, I found myself thinking about him a lot. I started to attend a bereavement support group, and I heard a lot of personal stories. Some of the people in that group were just like me and had also recently lost someone close. But some of the group members had attended for years. They saw it as part of their duty to their own loved ones to pass along their stories and encourage others to tell theirs. Part of the group was dedicated to members talking about how they'd been affected by their loss and how they felt. The rest of the evening was set aside to talk about the lives of those who had died.

That set me thinking. Although he'd had only a short life——he was in his twenties when he died of cancer——I realized there was a lot more to Paul's life than just his death. Paul was the product, even when he died, of an entire life, even if it was cut short. Paul's death, as unfair as it was, shaped the way Paul saw the world and the things he did right up until he passed away.

At first, I just listened to other people's remembrances. After a while, though, I decided to use that time in group to tell Paul's story—the story of his life and his death. Telling Paul's story has brought great relief to me.

IN OTHER CHAPTERS, you've written about your loss; your relationship with others; personal meaning; and other thoughts, feelings, and reactions to the death of a loved one. In some ways, though, these things are all secondary—they follow the fact that you had a relationship with a *person*. Although that relationship took on a life and direction of its own, it could never have existed without your loved one. And as you work through your grief, you also have to take the time to explore that relationship and the other person in it—your loved one. The journal entries in this chapter will help you think about and explore aspects of who that person *was*—the life and times of your loved one.

The Obituary: Recording a Life Past

Strictly speaking, a biography is a history of someone's life, written by another person. A meaningful biography is not simply a collection of facts and details. Rather, it contains important elements that tell the reader something about who the subject of the biography was *as a person*. It's a history of a life that offers a glimpse inside that person's life and thoughts, and in this way it is an exploration of a life lived rather than simply a record of it.

An obituary is a special form of biography that presents a brief public record of a loss. It contains information about a life now passed, capturing and freezing that life in print and in time. When people who are bereaved write obituaries, they do so to commemorate the deceased, to inform others of their loss, and to offer the world a testimonial about their loved one. Writing an obituary is an expression of sorrow, love, and honor.

What would you want people to know about the life of your loved one? Would you want them to know only his or her very best facets, or would you want to share the idiosyncrasies and human side of your loved one? Perhaps you'd write an obituary that outlined the life story, complete with dates, places, people, and accomplishments. Or maybe you might choose to focus on only one aspect of your loved one's life, such as his or her friendships, career, interests, or those things bequeathed to others in death.

In an obituary, *what* you say and *how* you say it speaks not only of the deceased but also of what she or he meant to others. In this next journal entry you will think about and write an obituary.

What you decide to do with this obituary is entirely up to you. You may choose to simply keep it in your journal. Or you can share it with people in your circle of support. If you prefer, you can actually submit it to a local newspaper. Whatever your eventual choice, write it as though it was intended for others to read.

In an obituary, what you say and how you say it speaks not only of the deceased but also of what she or he meant to others.

I WANT THE WORLD TO KNOW . . .

Think first about what you want to say in an obituary. What do you want other people to know about your loved one? Do you want to write about only the facts and details of your loved one's life, or do you want to present a more intimate view that tells others who the deceased was in your life and what your loved one meant to others?

Look through obituaries in your local newspaper. Get a sense of how they read, the sort of things people write about their losses, and how they make you feel reading them. Begin with the basics of any biography: dates, places, and other important details that record a life and death.

1. Name of your loved one: _____

Birth date: _____ Date of death: _____

Place of birth: _____

2. Other important details which may include marriages, births, and achievements:

_____

_____

_____

_____

3. Write the obituary.

_____

_____

_____

_____

_____

_____

_____

_____

_____

_____

THINGS TO THINK ABOUT

- What was it like to commit to paper the details of your loved one's death: the name, dates, and other information? Was it difficult, or did it further help to relieve feelings for you?

- Did you feel satisfied with the obituary you wrote? Did it say and express the things you wanted it to?

- Will the obituary be a "keeper"—something you keep private and never share, or will you consider submitting to a local publication?

The Biography: Recording a Life Lived

Although an obituary is a form of biography, what you write and the amount you write are somewhat dictated by space limitations. As you move beyond the obituary, you have the opportunity to write a more complete biography, limited only by the way you viewed the life that was lived and by the boundaries you set for yourself. Where an obituary is primarily intended as a record of a death, a biography is a record of a life—often, a celebration of that life.

Because of its intimate nature, a biography is as much about the writer as the subject. Any biography you write presents a portrait of you as well as the deceased—what *you* saw in your loved one, what *you* choose to write about, how your loved one affected *you,* and how *you* elected to present the deceased in his or her biography.

As you face the task of writing about the deceased, you have to ask yourself this question: who was your loved one? Just as there are many sides to you, there were many sides to your loved one also. She or he filled many different roles in life and probably looked very different to different people at different times. And, quite probably, your own view of your loved one changed from day to day. On some occasions, you may have seen him or her as warm, supportive, and understanding. On other days, she or he may have seemed distant, harsh, or inconsiderate. The direction of any biography written by you will largely depend on your point of view at the time of writing.

Of course, a biography can be written from lots of angles; quite likely, someone else writing a biography of your loved one will write something completely different from yours. That is because your loved one was not unidimensional. As you continue moving through your grief work, it is important that you neither idealize nor pigeonhole your loved one or your relationship. Just

"Tears are sometimes an inappropriate response to death. When a life has been lived completely honestly, completely successfully, or just completely, the correct response to death's perfect punctuation mark is a smile."
—JULIE BURCHILL

as you saw him or her in life, you need to see your loved one in death as a person with many sides.

In the next entry, you'll give yourself just ten minutes to compose a biographical sketch of your loved one's life. You may later decide to write a more complete account of his or her life, but for now you'll focus only on what can be written in a few minutes. This will require limiting yourself to a particular point of view about your loved one, a particular aspect of her or his life, or only a few facts that you see as most important for this biography. For instance, you can write about your loved one's personal history, personal qualities, general life experiences, specific life-shaping events or circumstances, or life choices.

You can describe your loved one's life in any way you want. You can focus on his or her entire life or on a single moment within it. You can shape the biography around one aspect of your loved one's life, or you can write a free-flowing biography that takes whatever direction pops into your head.

As you continue moving through your grief work, it is important that you neither idealize nor pigeonhole your loved one or your relationship.

A TEN-MINUTE BIOGRAPHY

1. Take a few minutes to think about how to write this biography and what aspect of your loved one's life to focus on. Some possibilities include:

_____ entire life   _____ career choices   _____ family influences

_____ childhood history   _____ adolescence   _____ early adulthood

_____ school years   _____ relationships   _____ shaping incidents

other: _____

_____

_____

2. Spend the next ten minutes writing a biography of your loved one's life from whichever perspective you've chosen.

_____

_____

_____

_____

_____

_____

_____

_____

_____

_____

_____

_____

_____

_____

_____

_____

_____

_____

_____

_____

_____

_____

3. What does the biography you've written say about you—the way you feel and the way you see your loved one today?

_____

_____

_____

_____

_____

4. What most influenced your choice of biography?

_____

_____

_____

_____

_____

5. If you wrote another biography, would it be different? Would you focus on the same material, or would you choose another slice of your loved one's life?

_____

_____

_____

_____

_____

THINGS TO THINK ABOUT

- Was it easy to write a biography, or was it difficult to find the material to write about? If it was difficult, why?
- Was it satisfying to write this brief biography? Will you later want to write a longer biography?

Character Sketching

In the biography you just wrote, you described the life—or part of the life—of your loved one. But even a biography can miss the *qualities* of the person you're writing about—those things that made your loved one the person he or she was.

As the name suggests, a character sketch is a brief "snapshot." It's an impression, a thumbnail profile, a quick view that captures and conveys the essence of someone. What kind of person was your loved one? What were his or her special qualities, oddities, or flaws? What were the things about your loved one that made him or her special? In this next entry, you'll create a quick sketch of your loved one.

A QUICK SKETCH

1. *My loved one was . . .* _____

_____

2. *The thing that was most special about my loved one was . . .* _____

_____

3. *The thing that most bothered me about my loved one was . . .* _____

_____

4. *My loved one's best qualities were . . .* _____

_____

5. *My loved one's most obvious flaws were . . .* _____

_____

6. *The most unusual or the oddest thing about my loved one was . . .* _____

_____

7. Describe your loved one. _____

_____

_____

_____

_____

_____

_____

_____

_____

_____

THINGS TO THINK ABOUT

- Was it difficult to think about your loved one in small character "chunks"? Was it easier to think about the special qualities, or did your loved one's flaws come to mind first?
- Did the character sketch help you present an accurate portrait of your loved one?
- Is your view of your loved one balanced? Do some aspects tend to stand out more clearly than others? Is this okay?

What We Own Is What We Are

There's more to your loved one than what you can write in a short biography or a brief character sketch. As you recollect your loved one's personality and history, and try to capture these memories and thoughts in your journal, think about some of his or her other defining features—those things that were *reflections* of your loved one, such as recreational activities, the choice of clothing, or the kind of photographs and pictures put up around the house. These things are *indirect* representations of your loved one. They are the mirrors of your loved one's life. The essence is captured in the things he or she chose to be surrounded with. That's why a favorite briefcase, an old stuffed animal, a favorite book, or a collection of comics become so important after a death. They not only represent and remind us of the deceased, but they also become cherished items that somehow *embody* part of our loved one.

Perhaps nothing says more about a person than the things he or she collects and chooses to keep. The things we own and prize exemplify our choices—our decision that these particular objects have value to us. You can learn a lot about people by thinking about what they own. What was important to your loved one? What can you learn about your loved one by thinking about a favorite possession? What does this favored item say about your loved one, and how can this prized object help you fondly remember a loved one?

As you recollect your loved one's personality and history, and try to capture these memories and thoughts in your journal, think about some of his or her other defining features—those things that were reflections of your loved one.

AN IMPORTANT POSSESSION

Pick something that was one of your loved one's most prized possessions prior to his or her death. It doesn't have to be something that your loved one treated in a special way or proclaimed to be cherished; it can simply be something that was clearly important because of the way your loved one treated or used it. It might be a favorite chair or desk, a book, or a worn article of clothing. It could be an award or trophy, a painting, or a pen. It might even be the television remote control.

Pick one favorite inanimate item (rather than a pet, for instance). Through this favorite possession, explore the life of your loved one. Why was this item so important? What did this choice say about your loved one? It may even be true that your loved one's favored possessions weren't flattering. But the idea in this entry is to remember and cope, not idealize or sanctify.

1. Decide which prized objects in your loved one's life were among the most important to her or him. Imagine that in death, your loved one could have taken one of these possessions along. Which would it be?

2. If it is available to you, go and get that object now and place it in front of you. If it's too large to move, go to it. Look at it carefully. Study its shape, its texture, and its qualities. Think about what it meant to your loved one, and why.

3. Why was this object so important to your loved one?

_____

_____

_____

4. What does this prized possession say about your loved one?

_____

_____

_____

5. Is there anything appealing to you about this possession? Does it have any extra meaning since your loss?

_____

_____

_____

6. Of all the objects that your loved one had, why did you pick this one?

_____

_____

_____

THINGS TO THINK ABOUT
- Were you surprised at how much you knew or how little you knew about the possessions most prized by your loved one?
- Did you learn anything about your loved one by considering the value of this object to her or him?
- Does this item carry fond reminders for you? Does it leave bad feelings for you? If so, is this part of unfinished business?

Other Recollections

Doubtless, there are many more things that can be said about your loved one, many more things for you to reflect on about her or his life, and much more to be learned about who your loved one was.

In this chapter, you wrote a ten-minute biography. But there are many other sides to your loved one, and many other ways to see and write about his or her life. Consider writing some of these "other" biographies—life stories that you write on different days and from different perspectives. In this way, you wind up with a biography that consists of many smaller biographies. Or you may decide to one day tackle writing a complete biography that encompasses many aspects of your loved one's life.

You may find creating a physical record of this life quite comforting. Biographies are just one means of exploring, remembering, and recording a life. In the next chapters, you will continue working through some of these memories and issues, and you will have the chance to keep focusing on the meaning of your loved one's life, the impact of that life on your own, and keeping the memory and lessons learned alive.

CHECKPOINT: BIOGRAPHY

1. What has been the most useful part of writing your loved one's biography?

_____

_____

_____

_____

_____

_____

2. As you complete this chapter, what needs to be said about your loved one that hasn't already been said?

_____

_____

_____

_____

3. There are many biographies about your loved one. In this chapter, you wrote just one. Are there other biographies of your loved one that you'd write? If so, outline one or two ideas here to return to later.

_____

_____

_____

_____

4. Are there people with whom you want to share what you've written here?

_____

_____

_____

_____

5. As you complete this chapter and its journal entries, how do you feel?

_____

_____

_____

_____

_____

THINGS TO THINK ABOUT

- The work in your grief journal is largely "internal." Do you need to be more "external"—sharing with others what you're writing, feeling, thinking, and learning? If you're already sharing, are you satisfied that you're sharing with the right people?

- Are there others who are sharing your loss who might benefit by doing their own grief work?

11

Destination:
RECORDING YOUR SHARED HISTORY

*"If we could know
Which of us, darling,
    would be the first
    to go,
Who would be first to
    breast the swelling
    tide
And step alone upon
    the other side—
If we could know!"*
—JULIA HARRIS MAY

SALLY

*My cousin Sasha and I grew up together and were very close when
we were young. We were only six months apart in age, and we were
both named for our grandmother Sarah. We looked alike and grew
up feeling and acting like sisters as well as best friends.*

*In our teens and early adulthood we grew apart, but in our late
twenties we found each other again. It was wonderful—like redis-
covering a long-lost twin sister. We had so much to remember and
talk about, and we developed a whole new relationship. But after
only a couple of years, Sasha died suddenly from a cerebral hemor-
rhage, and she was gone, just like that.*

*I felt heartbroken and became quite disconsolate. I hadn't really
realized how much I'd missed Sasha during those years we weren't
together, until she was taken away again. Even though I have my
own family now, I feel like part of me is missing—a part I can't
seem to recapture. Sasha was part of my history.*

JUST AS THERE'S a history behind every person, the same is true
for every relationship. This book—your journal—is about

both. It's a history of your loved one and what she or he meant to you, and it's a history of your relationship. In fact, every entry in this journal is about your loved one and about you.

You may not have realized that, above all, you've been dealing with relationship issues as you've been working through your grief and developing your journal. In many ways, it is the loss of the relationship that you are grieving.

Recording Your Relationship

The word *relationship* is used to describe any affiliation among people, but people can also have relationships with their jobs, their cars, and the things they do. When used in its most significant sense, however, a relationship implies an emotional connection and a bond.

Although there are many types of relationships among people, only a few contain intimate meaning for each of the people in it. These can probably be boiled down to the sort of relationships that exist between parents, children, other close family members, romantic partners, and friends. In these sorts of relationships, there's a sense of shared lives and often linked destinies. What affects one person in the relationship affects the other. This is true of the relationship you had with your loved one. This is why you grieve.

The "togetherness" implied by your relationship doesn't require a physical closeness—just an emotional connection.

This journal is a chronicle of your thoughts, feelings, and experiences since the death of your loved one. But it is also a record of your life *together*. "Together," though, doesn't mean you were "in each other's pockets." If you and your loved one were spouses, you may have been with one another daily. But if your loved one was an adult child, sibling, or friend, you may have lived halfway across the country and had little direct contact before his or her death. The "togetherness" implied by your relationship doesn't require a physical closeness—just an emotional connection. It's this emotional bond that sealed your relationship.

As you create and develop your journal, you're writing a biography of your loved one, part of your own life, and your relationship.

OUR RELATIONSHIP

As you complete this journal entry, you'll answer each question in ways that fit *your* relationship. For instance, if you're writing about your parent, your answers will be very different than if you're writing about a loved one who was your romantic partner.

1. Describe your relationship.

_____

_____

_____

_____

_____

_____

2. Where did you meet?

_____

3. How did you meet?

_____

_____

_____

_____

4. What brought you and your loved one together?

_____

_____

_____

_____

5. What bonded you and your loved one?

_____

_____

_____

_____

6. What kept you together?

_____

_____

_____

_____

7. What was the most important part of your relationship?

_____

_____

_____

_____

_____

8. *Our relationship was . . .* _____

_____

_____

_____

_____

_____

_____

The next question is one that you can complete repeatedly. In this entry, pick only one important memory. Then think about other important memories that you may want to write about, and complete this portion of the entry again.

9. Recall and describe one important memory of your early relationship.

_____

_____

_____

_____

_____

_____

_____

_____

_____

_____

THINGS TO THINK ABOUT

- Was it easy or difficult to answer the questions about what bonded you and what kept you together? Did you already know what connected you both, or did this entry help crystallize it?
- Has thinking about your relationship and your bonds left you with unanswered questions? If so, what can you do to get answers?
- Some of the questions may have seemed obvious, for instance, Where did you meet? But was it easy to answer these "obvious" questions, or did you find "blanks" in your memories?
- Are there important early memories you want to spend more time recalling or writing about?

Special Days

There are many reasons to look back on your history: the recollection of shared friends and family, good and sad times, turning points in your life, and the memory of lessons learned that help you in your life today. In your shared history, there were many important days too: the day you met, an event fondly remembered, a proud achievement, or a special dinner.

Since the death of your loved one, you may have come to feel that *every* day you spent together was special. It would be wonderful to be able to recall and treasure every day as eventful or distinctive, but for most people that's not the case. But there are days and times that do stand out as special, and these are not easily forgotten. These days are enormously important, because they are the days of your life. Although every day in a life together is a shared day, many are routine and taken for granted; these fall into distant memory or are simply forgotten. The days that stand out, though, are the days that can be relished. In some cases, they are the good days—the fun times, the accomplishments, the special event or celebration. In other cases, the memories aren't so good—a shattered dream or dashed hope, a disappointment, sad news. If the death of your loved one was expected, this certainly includes the day you both learned of his or her impending death.

When you think of these days—the days when you together *shared that moment or that experience—you're recollecting your history together.*

When you think of these days—the days when you *together* shared that moment or that experience—you're recollecting your history together. Part of grief work is recalling these moments so that they can sustain you or instruct you as you work your way through your current life.

AN IMPORTANT DAY

Think of a day with your loved one that stands out in your memory. The day can be important for any number of reasons. It could be a fun day or an awful one. It could be a milestone for one or both of you or for another member of your shared family, or it could be a turning point in your relationship. Or it could be a day that you spent together that simply stands out because of the weather or where you happened to be. The day could be a momentous occasion or just a fast-food meal shared together. It doesn't matter if it's a memory of a good day or a difficult time. What counts here is that the day has significance in your shared history.

1. List six important "good" days.

a. _____   d. _____

b. _____   e. _____

c. _____   f. _____

2. List six important "bad" days.

a. _____   d. _____

b. _____   e. _____

c. _____   f. _____

3. Pick one of these days—good or bad—as the focus of this journal entry. You can repeat the entry again for each of the other days on your list.

_____

_____

4. Describe this important day.

_____

_____

_____

_____

_____

_____

5. *I chose to write about this day because . . .* _____

_____

6. *This day is important in our history because . . .* _____

_____

_____

7. *The most important thing about this day is . . .* _____

_____

_____

8. *As I think of this day, it makes me feel* . . . _____

_____

_____

_____

_____

9. *As I relive this day now, I realize that* . . . _____

_____

_____

_____

THINGS TO THINK ABOUT

- What was it like to recall this day? How did it leave you feeling?
- Is there a lesson learned from this day?
- Is it important to remember these days? Will you write about the other special days in your shared history?
- Are there people in your life today with whom you should count every day as special?

Anniversaries and Milestones—Relationship Landmarks

Some important days are especially significant because they mark a change. Perhaps something new was introduced into your life. Maybe the day marked the end of one phase of your life and the beginning of a new one. Whatever the particular significance, something changed on that day.

These are landmark days and are usually remembered for years to come as special days, sometimes as anniversaries of one kind or another and sometimes as milestones—markers in your life that tell you how far you've come. In relationships, landmarks come in all forms.

Anniversaries are usually annual celebrations of a special event within a relationship. Birthdays are one example, especially first, seventh, thirteenth, sixteenth, and twenty-first birthdays, depending on religion and culture. Anniversaries can also be marked by the number of years spent together as a romantic couple, a return to an old vacation spot year after year, or other events shared annually. Milestones, in contrast, might include a college graduation, a first job, or a first home bought and shared.

The most important part of these days is that they were landmarks for you both within your shared history. And, depending on your relationship, the landmarks may include other people as well, such as family members and close friends.

Like the important days you wrote about in the previous entry, these days mark your relationship; they are days to be cherished and remembered as part of what you'll always have with your loved one, because they're embedded in your memory.

LIFE MARKERS

Think about those special days that were landmarks in your relationship. First think of three milestone events—days or times that you look back on as turning points in your relationship or in the history that you shared with your loved one. Then consider three anniversaries—days that marked a moment when something special happened that you commemorated on a regular basis in your relationship from that day on.

1. Milestones. Why were these days significant, and what made them milestones for each of you?

a. Milestone: _____ Date: _____

Significance: _____

_____

This milestone is important to me because . . . _____

_____

_____

This milestone was important to my loved one because . . . _____

_____

_____

b. Milestone:_____ Date: _____

Significance: _____

_____

This milestone is important to me because . . . _____

_____

_____

This milestone was important to my loved one because . . . _____

_____

_____

c. Milestone: _____ Date: _____

Significance: _____

_____

This milestone is important to me because . . . _____

_____

_____

This milestone was important to my loved one because . . . _____

_____

_____

2. Anniversaries. What did these anniversaries commemorate, and why?

a. Anniversary: _____

Date:_____ Celebrating _____ years

This anniversary was important to us because . . . _____

_____

_____

In our relationship, this anniversary meant . . . _____

_____

_____

b. Anniversary: _____

Date: _____ Celebrating _____ years

This anniversary was important to us because . . . _____

_____

_____

In our relationship, this anniversary meant . . . _____

_____

_____

c. Anniversary: _____

Date: _____ Celebrating _____ years

This anniversary was important to us because . . . _____

_____

_____

In our relationship, this anniversary meant . . . _____

_____

_____

3. Are there other important landmarks, turning points, or dates in your shared history? Name them.

_____

_____

4. How did landmarks such as these help build and seal your relationship?

_____

_____

_____

- What would your relationship have been like without milestones, anniversaries, and other landmarks? Is it possible to have a meaningful relationship without shared landmarks?
- Can you continue to celebrate important milestones and anniversaries, even though your loved one is deceased?

Outlasting Grief

"Man sheds grief as his skin sheds rain."
—RALPH WALDO EMERSON

You grieve not only the loss of someone important but also the loss of a relationship. Unlike the irreplaceable loss of your loved one, however, the relationship you had can never be truly lost, because it lives on in you. Keeping your memories and the spirit of your relationship alive is that part of the healing process that outlasts the grief you have felt and are feeling still.

Your relationship will always reside in your memory and history. It will be important for you to find comfort, warmth, and encouragement in your shared history and to draw both strength and lessons learned from that history.

I'LL NEVER FORGET

1. *I'll never forget when we . . .* _____

_____

_____

2. *I'll never forget when you . . .* _____

_____

_____

3. *I'll never forget when we first . . .* _____

_____

_____

4. *I'll never forget . . .* _____

_____

_____

5. *I'll never forget . . .* _____

_____

_____

6. *I'll never forget . . .* _____

_____

_____

THINGS TO THINK ABOUT

- Does your relationship live on in your memory? Have you been able to find that relationship still living inside of you?
- Who else is part of your shared history—family or friends? Can you keep drawing support from these other people? Do they need to keep drawing support from you?

12

Destination:
REMEMBRANCES AND COMMEMORATIONS

PATRICK

Steve was a really beloved guy who worked with kids at the community center. His death was a surprise to us all and an especially difficult blow to everyone who knew him because he died at work.

The funeral was incredible—two school buses brought dozens of kids, parents, and teachers, who joined Steve's family and friends for the services. After the burial, testimonies were read, many of them written and read by kids, and this really helped us all. I got to read a memorial I'd written myself and shared my thoughts, and I found a lot of relief in hearing the memories of others. I know the memorial service helped Steve's family also, especially his own children, who saw how much people thought of their dad.

Every year now, on the anniversary of Steve's death, we commemorate his passing with a tree planting on the grounds of the center. Of course, we're all getting older now, but it's still a really special event for many of us, and there's always a big turnout. Steve's wife and kids are always there. The annual event has lost its sadness now and has become a wonderful way not only to remember Steve but to get together—and that was what Steve was all about!

DURING THIS MIDDLE stage of grief, you've become deeply immersed in the reality of your loss and the changes it's brought to your life. As you work toward containing, understanding, and expressing your sorrow, memories will continually pop in and out of your thoughts, shaping and affecting your feelings.

However, just as the end of mourning isn't marked by the absence of feelings, it isn't marked by the end of memory either. And we would not want it to be. Memories are an important tool in your recovery—they help to keep your relationship alive and help you deal with your grief. As you move through your grief, you'll find that your memories are not only sad—perhaps overwhelmingly so at first—but also increasingly nostalgic.

Memories are an important tool in your recovery—they help to keep your relationship alive and help you deal with your grief.

Memories, Commemoration, and Nostalgia

It's true that memories can make you wince, sadden you, and remind you of the things you've lost. But they can also provide comfort and make you smile. Just as you use your journal to express your thoughts and feelings, you can use it to capture the memories that provide the warmth of nostalgia. In fact, this is often one of the prime reasons that journals are used in the first place—to capture, explore, and record memories.

Memories keep the past alive and link your present to your past. For some people, especially those who have experienced trauma, memories are difficult things to deal with, disturbing and intrusive. Nevertheless, even in these cases the goal isn't to erase memory but instead to learn to control it. If you find that your memories are too difficult to deal with, or you have only disturbing memories, you may require outside help to learn how to tolerate, manage, and filter them.

For most people, though, memories serve to positively connect their present to their past. They allow us to remember lessons learned and to recall past pleasures of all kinds. On a broader scale, societies memorialize the past through commemoration, rituals, symbols, and other ceremonies that serve to remind us of or celebrate the past. Where commemoration stands as a *formal* monument to the past, nostalgia is that *personal* aspect of memory that captures the warmth and pleasure of the past. Both serve important roles in grief work.

Through memorials and other commemorations, you can recall and pay tribute to that which has past. This is a powerful way to say good-bye to the past while paying tribute to it and keeping its memory alive. In grieving, there are all sorts of commemorations, from the funeral service and other ceremonies that immediately follow the death to the later dedication of cemetery headstones to the annual lighting of commemorative candles. These sorts of dedications are usually prescribed by social or religious customs.

It is important that your relationship with the deceased be based on nostalgia; it should not be a relationship that prevents you from moving on with your life and your living relationships.

Nostalgia has a special power too. It allows us to look back in fondness and enjoy the past, even if we will miss it. It is through this fond recall that memories promote healing, allowing us to revisit the past and draw inspiration and courage to face the present. The loss of memory is one of the most crushing ailments imaginable because it places us only in the present, leaving us stranded without the benefit of past wisdom, experience, and inspiration.

Keeping Memory Alive

With the passing of your loved one, the living relationship you had ended. But this doesn't mean you no longer have a relationship. Nor does it mean you shouldn't have one. The question is, what kind of relationship? As you move on with your life, it will become more and more important to work on the relationships you currently have—with children, family, friends, and others—and build and develop new relationships. It is important, then, that your relationship with the deceased be based on nostalgia; it should not be a relationship that prevents you from moving on with your life and your living relationships.

Using a Journal for Memories

There are many ways to memorialize your relationship. In this chapter, you'll use your journal as one way to record and explore memories. You may wish to photocopy blank journal entries before you complete them so that you can reuse the entry for different memories. Or you may want to maintain a separate blank journal in which you can complete individual journal entries repeatedly, without space limitations. In some cases, you'll do journal work outside of the space provided here and use the journal entry in this book to describe and reflect on your work or as a general journal format that you can repeat in a separate journal.

Memories as Stories

No doubt, there were many people who knew and cared for your loved one in different ways: as family, friends, colleagues, or peers, for example. Besides your own memories and stories of your loved one, many of the people in this larger community probably have their fond memories as well. Some of their stories you know already, but there may be many more to be told and shared. Each of these stories can be told, and in so doing you have the opportunity to tell and record the tales of your loved one's life and to look back and reminisce.

This next entry is a little different. It connects you with others in that larger community. In a way it's an exercise in journalism, as it requires you to ask others about *their* memories, in addition to thinking about your own. You may have heard some of these stories before. You may have even shared them with others during the services and ceremonies after the funeral—at a wake, perhaps, or while sitting shivah. For this entry, you'll be collecting some of these stories. At first, it may seem a little awkward to be asking about and collecting tales and reminiscences about your loved one, but here you're really compiling stories about his or her life. In this way, you're not only reliving and recording memories but also commemorating the life of your loved one, told through your own memories and those of others.

You may only use one story—perhaps your own or perhaps a story from someone else—but if you find the process satisfying and important, you'll be able to compile many stories that become a legacy to keep forever and pass along.

TELLING TALES

For this entry, think of fond memories—things or stories about your loved one that stand out in your mind and bring back good memories.

1. Besides yourself, who else has stories to tell—who else knows your loved one well enough to tell their own tales?

_____   _____

_____   _____

_____   _____

_____   _____

2. Talk to four of these people, and from each gather three stories.

3. For this entry pick one tale to tell. Whose story is this?

_____

4. Why did you pick this story for this entry?

_____

_____

5. Had you heard this story before you gathered it for this entry? What was it like to hear the story for the first time or to hear or tell it again?

_____

_____

6. Describe the story.

_____

_____

_____

_____

_____

_____

_____

THINGS TO THINK ABOUT

• What was compiling this entry like for you? Was it uncomfortable at first, or did it come easily and naturally?
• Was it easy or difficult to find stories to be told? Are there more stories to tell?
• Whose tale did you tell for this entry—your own or someone else's? Why did you make that choice?
• Will you share these stories with anyone else as you compile them?

Memorabilia

There are other ways to remember and "freeze" your memories. There are many aspects of your loved one's life that exist and through which memories can easily be evoked—photographs, favorite possessions, awards, letters, and so on.

Memorabilia are tangible things that remind you of something. For instance, airline ticket stubs from a trip you once took may bring back a flood of memories. A collection of old records when played again can evoke the memories of a certain day or time in your life; you're almost certain to have had the experience of hearing a piece of music or smelling an odor and being transported back to that time in your life. Memories are locked up in the memorabilia you keep. Mementos become an important part of your life, a collection of your memories.

For this reason, memorabilia of your loved one can be an important aspect of keeping memory and relationship alive. Collecting the things that capture memory and represent your loved one can prove soothing at times. At other times, they serve to bring a smile to your face or simply remind you of a day spent together.

One time-honored way to collect and preserve the mementos, keepsakes, and souvenirs of someone's life is through a scrapbook. There are many ways to keep a memory book, but most often it will contain a collection of the things that are the most important or most typical reminders of the person whose life is featured: photos, newspaper clippings, awards, favorite poems, writing, letters, artwork, and anything else that can be included in a book or somehow attached to it.

For this next entry, you'll create a scrapbook of memorabilia. Of course, the entry, by design, can't *be* the memory book. Instead, through the entry explore the idea of a memorabilia scrapbook and how to develop one. As for the book itself, it can be a purchased item or something you create yourself. It can be small or big, made up of white paper or colored paper, thick or thin. You can add things that you already have or you can search out items to include. Over time, you can continually add to your book of memories, by adding your own thoughts, artwork, and writings. In this way, your memory book itself becomes both an act of creation and commemoration, and an extension of your journal.

Memorabilia of your loved one can be an important aspect of keeping memory and relationship alive.

A SCRAPBOOK

1. What sort of memorabilia exists that can be easily gathered and placed in or attached to a memory book? Add ideas of your own.

_____ artwork   _____ awards   _____ certificates

_____ favorite poems   _____ insignia   _____ jewelry

_____ letters   _____ music   _____ newspaper clippings

_____ photographs   _____ ticket stubs   _____ writing

other:

_____ _____

_____ _____

_____ _____

2. What other things remind you of your loved one but can't fit into a scrapbook?

_____ _____

_____ _____

_____ _____

_____ _____

3. Is there some way to creatively attach some of these other mementos or make reference to them so that they can be included in your memory book?

_____

_____

4. What are some things you can create yourself—such as poems, drawings, or collages—that will help you remember certain aspects of your loved one or certain days in your life together?

_____ _____

_____ _____

_____ _____

_____ _____

5. Are there things that you can collect from other people that can be included in your book of memories?

_____   _____

_____   _____

_____   _____

_____   _____

6. Write an introduction to your memory book.

_____

_____

_____

_____

_____

_____

THINGS TO THINK ABOUT

- Will your memory book be an ongoing work where you continually add material, or will you stop after its initial creation? How will you know the "right" amount of memorabilia to include in your scrapbook?
- Is it comforting to create a memory book, or is it difficult at this time? Will the way you use a memory book change over time? Will the type of memorabilia you add differ as you work through your grief and more fully reclaim and move on with your life?

Visiting the Past

You and your loved one shared experiences—people you knew, places you went, and things you did together. In this sense, you had a shared history, some of which you explored through the journal entries in the previous chapter. If you didn't have a common history, you most likely wouldn't be experiencing grief at this time. Of course, the sort of experiences shared depend on your relationship—whether you were a child, parent, sibling, spouse, or close friend of the deceased.

Whatever your relationship, there were people, experiences, and events in your life that you had in common up until the time of the death. But there are also bound to be people, places, and things from your past together—from your shared history. The people might include a relative long absent from your life, an old friend, or a work colleague. The places could be an old house, a vacation spot, a favorite nature trail, a museum, or a school once attended. The things might be a favorite old movie, a sports event, a painting, a park bench in your old neighborhood, or a walk through that old neighborhood. In each case, these are things from your past together, each of which has locked within it vivid memories of your relationship and times gone by. It's often nostalgic to revisit the past under any circumstances, but it can be especially poignant when such a visit helps you to feel close to and still in touch with your loved one and those things you've shared.

The next two entries are directly linked. In the first, think about those people, places, and things from the past and the memories attached to them. Then, if possible, pay a visit to that past experience, and in the second entry write about the memories evoked. These entries are intended to be repeated, so either make photocopies of the blank entries or make additional entries in a separate notebook.

A TRIP IN TIME

1. Name three people from the past you shared with your loved one. These can be relatives, friends, old roommates, or schoolteachers—anyone who is still alive but not an active part of your current life. Name only people who evoke special memories of your relationship with your loved one.

a. _____

b. _____

c. _____

2. Name three places from your shared past. These can include places you lived, places you visited frequently, or places you visited infrequently or just once. Name only places from your shared past that carry with them strong memories of your relationship.

a. _____

b. _____

c. _____

3. Name three things you used to do together—not in your life immediately prior to the death, but from your past. Think about activities you used to share like long walks, eating popcorn and watching an old movie, or watching the stars together at night. Once again, think about only those that have special memories attached of times spent together.

a. _____

b. _____

c. _____

Pick one of these people, places, or things. The rest of this entry will focus only on that choice. This is an entry that you can repeat for each of the people, places, and things you've named above.

4. Who, where, or what have you chosen for the entry?

_____

5. What special memories are attached?

_____

_____

_____

_____

_____

_____

- What's it like to recollect this aspect of your shared past?
- Is there some reason you can't revisit this person, place, or thing?
- What might it be like to revisit? What does it feel like to even consider a visit?

Back from the Future

Now pay a visit to the person, place, or thing you've chosen. Ideally, make your visit in person, if this is possible. If a direct visit isn't possible and you've chosen a person, make a phone call, write a letter, or find some other way to get in contact. If you've chosen a place or thing to revisit, but can't go in person, look at old photos or other mementos that allow vivid recollection.

A VISIT THROUGH TIME

1. Describe your visit.

_____

_____

_____

_____

2. What memories did it bring back?

_____

_____

_____

_____

3. What feelings were evoked for you?

_____

_____

_____

4. In what ways did your visit affect your sense of shared history or connect you to your loved one?

_____

_____

5. How did this visit to the past leave you feeling?

_____

THINGS TO THINK ABOUT

- Will you consider visiting with this person, place, or thing again? Has this trip affected your plans to visit other people, places, or things?
- What was the best part about this visit? What was the most difficult part?
- Is there someone you can share these memories and experiences with? Who, and what will that be like? If not, why not?

Commemoration

Until now, you've been using your journal to experience, reflect on, and record personal memories. But commemoration is different—it's a formal way to keep your memories alive, mark your loss, and celebrate and remember the relationship you had. Unlike personal memories, commemorations are often made public. You share your loss and memories with others or at least make others aware of your loss. Of course, it's quite possible to have a commemoration that's private too.

Whether public or private, the difference between a memory and a commemoration is the formal, and usually ceremonial, nature of the memory. Commemoration typically involves an observance or ceremony of some kind—a planned statement to memorialize your loved one.

Many religions and cultures have formal and prescribed ways to commemorate loss, often at defined times and in specific

ways. For instance, the funeral itself is a commemorative ceremony, with most religious traditions prescribing when and how
the funeral takes place. The headstone provides a more permanent commemorative marker, memorializing the death and often
offering inspirational words. In some religions, there is a later
consecration of the headstone, accompanied by an additional
commemorative service. Religious and cultural ceremonies usually continue to follow the death over time, as in the lighting of
memorial candles, shrines, annual prayers, and other remembrances.

Some public holidays serve as broader commemorations to individuals or groups of individuals—Martin Luther King's birthday and Veterans Day, for example. These public occasions are
intended to memorialize not only individuals but also what they
stood for. You have an opportunity to memorialize your loss too
—not only in the formal ways that may be customary in your religion or culture but also in your own personal and unique way.
In considering a memorial, you have many options.

*You have an
opportunity to
memorialize your loss
too—not only in the
formal ways that may
be customary in your
religion or culture
but also in your own
personal and unique
way.*

- You may choose to individually design a commemoration
  alone, or you may choose to let others be part of the planning and creation of the memorial.

- Your commemoration may be strictly private, or it may involve others in the ceremonies that accompany the commemoration.

- The commemoration may involve a one-time ceremony, or
  it may be a ceremony or event that you repeat periodically,
  on an annual or other basis, for years to come.

- The memorial may be in the form of a one-time symbol
  such as a plaque or piece of artwork, or it may be ongoing
  and periodically renewed, such as annual gift giving or a se-
  ries of poems written over time.

- Your commemoration may be internal, involving ceremonies and services that affect only yourself and your immediate circle of family and friends. Or it may be external,
  designed to reach out and affect the lives of others, such as
  a charitable donation in the name of your loved one or a
  kind of public display (the planting of a tree or dedication of
  a bench in a local park or garden, for example).

- You may choose to memorialize your loss in formal ways that
  involve some sort of ceremony or ritual, or you may prefer
  to commemorate your loss informally, perhaps through an
  annual gathering of family and friends.

The ways to design and implement a commemoration are as var-
ied as the memorial itself. There is no correct way to design or
participate in a commemoration—the entire point is to help
you, and perhaps others in your circle, through your loss and beyond, and to leave you with a permanent marker of your loved
one.

In the end, the commemoration itself stands alone and lives
on, independent of and outside your memory. It will last long
after your grief has passed. In this way, the commemorative
memorial takes on a life of its own, serving to keep the meaning
of your relationship alive.

In Memoriam

Memorials and commemoration can take many forms. The bereaved have memorialized their losses in ways that range from
commissioning and erecting public statues and dedicating hospital wings to gathering with families each year to freely exchange
memories and stories to creating and compiling poetry and artwork. Some examples of commemorative acts include:

- making charitable donations
- creating a support group to help others
- dedicating a public gift, such as a park bench
- dedicating equipment to a school, hospital, or library
- gathering with family and friends
- planting a tree or flower garden
- creating poetry, artwork, or music to memorialize your loved one
- establishing a scholarship fund or foundation
- doing volunteer work

The way you choose to commemorate your loved one is limited only by your imagination and personal needs.

The last journal entry in this chapter will help you to think about how best a commemoration may meet your needs to remember your loved one and who may be most affected by the commemoration.

COMMEMORATING YOUR LOVED ONE

1. *I want a memorial to . . .* _____

_____

_____

_____

_____

2. *This commemoration will preserve . . .* _____

_____

_____

_____

_____

3. *This commemoration will celebrate . . .* _____

_____

_____

_____

_____

4. Who else will be directly affected by this memorial? Check off all the people who will be affected and moved by this commemoration, and add others not listed here. Next to each, briefly write how they will be affected.

_____ children   _____

_____ parents   _____

_____ siblings   _____

_____ in-laws   _____

_____ friends   _____

other:

_____ _____ _____

_____ _____ _____

_____ _____ _____

_____ _____ _____

_____ _____ _____

_____ no one else will be affected

5. What message do you most want this commemoration to give?

_____

_____

_____

_____

_____

- Is it important to have more than one kind of commemoration? Do you need one commemoration for yourself alone and another for others to share?
- Will you plan this memorial alone, or will you allow others to share in its design?

13

Destination:
RESOLVING UNFINISHED BUSINESS

BILLY

After Sheila died, I discovered that she'd had an affair just before her death. I found a letter she'd written to this other guy. In the letter, she said she was ending it with him because she realized she still loved me and wanted our relationship to work. Even though Sheila decided she loved me, it really doesn't make me feel much better. We'd had some problems, but I didn't know how bad things were between us. Now I feel like we were living a lie.

I know who this other guy is, but I don't know him well. Although I've seen him several times since I found out about their affair, I haven't said anything to him. Sometimes I want to yell at him, and sometimes I just want to know what happened. I have mixed feelings about what I want from him. I haven't talked to anyone else about this either, although I bet some of Sheila's friends knew about it. I'm too embarrassed, angry, and sad to talk about it, and I feel let down because no one told me. I'm just all wrapped up with it, and I feel like I can't get any peace now. Most of all, I want to talk to Sheila about it, because I can't get over my feelings. But I can't do that.

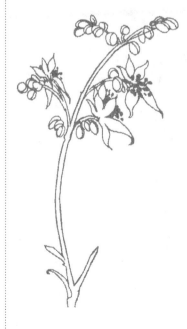

DAWN

Jerry passed away just before our fiftieth wedding anniversary. We had a big party planned with our children and friends, and then we were going on a sea cruise. You can imagine how I felt—the loss was terrible, and the emptiness that followed. But, in a way, the thing that felt the worse was we never got to celebrate our big moment together.

Well, you know, I celebrated our fiftieth anyway. Although, I didn't go on the cruise—that would have felt too strange—we had the party, and it was wonderful. *Nothing will bring back Jerry or take away the sting, but celebrating our fiftieth anyway sure felt good and helped me to say good-bye to my husband.*

WITH THE PASSING of your loved one, you may have been left with the feeling that much was left undone or unsaid. Part of you may even feel incomplete *because* something has been left undone in your relationship. But unlike other relationships that end, in the case of a death there's no chance for reconciliation, to go back and resolve unsettled issues, or to wish one another the best. With the sad reality of a death, the relationship ends—suddenly and forever.

But this irrevocable end doesn't mean that there aren't things that need to be addressed, resolved, and put to rest. The difference is, you have to find a way to put closure on the relationship on your own. The task is to come to terms with the uncompleted aspects of your relationship and move on.

Unfinished Business

The things you never did and the things you could have done differently. The words you should have said—or those you wish you'd never spoken. Those things you wanted to hear from your loved one but never did. The unresolved issues, differences, and feelings. The unfulfilled plans and expectations. This is the stuff of unfinished business.

People seek closure on the things in their life, and incompleteness can be a difficult thing to experience. If you briefly show someone a partial circle, with a small chunk missing, she or he may see it as a complete circle. The mind, seeking completion, sometimes fills in the part that's missing. In a chaotic world, people seek order and a sense of finality. Where there are holes—things missing—people strive to fill in the gap, sometimes in ways that are unhealthy and ineffective. The same is true for relationships.

In a chaotic world, people seek order and a sense of finality. . . . The same is true for relationships.

When a relationship ends, some people may have enormous difficulty letting go. Feelings of abandonment, insecurity, self-doubt, and self-blaming may create a barrier to their ability to move on. In such situations, the task is not to try to drown out the feelings or rekindle the relationship. Instead, the goal is to find ways to settle unresolved issues and become reconciled to reality. However, not everyone can do this. For those unable to resolve these sorts of issues, life can become an endless struggle of dealing with difficult feelings. People can become preoccupied with the relationship and their thoughts about it. They become emotionally stuck, unable to learn from the experience, build new relationships, and move on with their lives.

Following your loss, you may have unfinished business with your loved one. You may feel angry, guilty, resentful, or regretful. But with the death of your loved one, there is no one with whom to resolve these issues—except yourself.

Tying Up Loose Ends

How do you find resolution to an unresolvable situation? How do you undo something that has been irreversibly done? There is no way to *literally* reconcile and resolve issues and feelings between

There is no way to literally reconcile and resolve issues and feelings between you and your loved one. But you can redefine the problem and put it into a form that can *be resolved.*

you and your loved one. But you can redefine the problem and put it into a form that *can* be resolved.

The tasks in completing unfinished business include becoming self-expressive, contemplating, and letting go. These are personal tasks. When you complete them, you will have changed nothing in the world around you, and you will have changed no one else. But as you resolve unfinished business, you change yourself.

Tying up the loose ends first means identifying what those loose ends are—what business has been left incomplete. It also means recognizing that resolution is a state of mind, a perspective in which you are able to accept that which is unchangeable and through which you're able to explore and express feelings. In some regards, completing unfinished business is finding a way to say good-bye.

Once you're able to recognize what the loose ends are, you're in a position to figure out how best to tie them together. When loose ends are left to dangle, things eventually unravel further. But you can't simply pick up the pieces and neatly sew them back together. The way that you resolve unfinished business is through self-expression—finding ways to accept and relieve yourself of feelings by giving them a voice. By letting your feelings "speak," you rob them of the power to eat away at you.

Some of the things you say when you express your feelings may be difficult, and it may be hard to let them out. You may confess to being angry with your loved one for some reason or sorry because you didn't do enough for him or her before the death. Perhaps you feel responsible in some way for the death or guilty because you feel that your actions or inactions led to the death. Maybe you feel insecure and secretly wonder if your loved one loved you enough. These sorts of feelings are only one type of unfinished business, though. Another type is simple regret.

You may lament that you were unable to tell your loved one how much she or he meant to you, or you may be sad that you were unable to say good-bye the way you wanted to. Perhaps you mourn the fact that you didn't share something important before the death. Achieving closure may mean telling formerly untold secrets, sharing ideas never stated, apologizing for some injustice long gone by, or just saying good-bye.

Oddly enough, finding the strength to say the things that you need to say—finding a way to let go of these thoughts and feelings that will otherwise remain penned up inside of you—means that you'll have to learn how to relinquish self-control. Self-expression sometimes means letting go.

As difficult as it may be to speak out, as awkward as it may feel saying things to someone no longer present, your journal provides a private place in which you can work at your own pace, in your own time, and in your own way. Keep in mind that you're really voicing your thoughts out loud to yourself. The person you're resolving things with is *you*.

"I will indulge my sorrows, and give way To all the pangs and fury of despair."
— JOSEPH ADDISON

THINKING ABOUT UNFINISHED BUSINESS

In this entry, begin to think about the kinds of unfinished business in your life. Focus only on the *broad* issues you may have—don't worry about the details. Here, you're trying to look at your own thoughts and get in touch with your feelings, without focusing too deeply on the content and details of those thoughts or feelings.

The first question for you to ask yourself is, do you need closure on your relationship? Not everybody does. However, if you're this far into *The Healing Journey Through Grief,* chances are you have unresolved feelings and haven't figured out how to deal with them. Even if you don't feel that you need "deep" closure, or haven't much in the way of unfinished business, read through this entry and complete as much of it as fits.

1. Is the kind of closure you need more like saying good-bye and expressing your simple sorrow, or is it more like trying to vent deep feelings that have been left unresolved?

_____

_____

_____

_____

2. What kind of unfinished business do you have? Check all that apply, and add other types of unfinished business that you may have.

_____ unresolved feelings   _____ unshared experiences

_____ unexpressed thoughts   _____ unspoken words

_____ unstated regrets   _____ untold secrets

other: _____   _____

_____   _____

_____   _____

3. Of the things you checked off or added, which are about you—your thoughts and feelings, your actions, or your words? Which are about your loved one—his or her feelings, actions, or words?

Unfinished business about my actions, feelings, words, or thoughts includes . . . _____

_____

_____

_____

_____

Unfinished business about the actions, feelings, or words of my loved one includes . . . _____

_____

_____

_____

_____

4. Are your main issues about things done—things that you or your loved one did or said but perhaps shouldn't have? Or are they about things that were never done or said but perhaps should've been?

_____

_____

_____

_____

5. Tying up loose ends can be difficult and painful. What part will be the hardest for you?

_____

_____

_____

_____

6. What most concerns you as you think about resolving unfinished business?

_____

_____

_____

_____

7. Do you need to complete unfinished business? If so, why?

_____

_____

_____

_____

_____

_____

_____

Voicing Unresolved Feelings

In daily life, not every thought has to be explored, nor every feeling expressed. In social interactions, it's important to know what to say, when, and to whom. In your journal, these rules don't apply. Your journal is a place to explore everything, in whatever way you like. Although you may not feel comfortable voicing all of your thoughts and feelings—even to your closest friends—as you work through your grief, it will be important to do just this. In fact, one major purpose of a journal is to create that opportunity.

Finding the courage and honesty to name and give voice to difficult feelings is an important step on the journey to emotional healing.

Although you're certain to have strong, sometimes overpowering, feelings about your loss, it's important to realize that unfinished business is not about those feelings. Unfinished business is *strictly* about unresolved feelings connected to your loved one and your relationship. In *The Healing Journey Through Grief*, there are many opportunities for you to write about your feelings of loss, but the journal entries in this chapter call on you to focus solely on the unfinished business in your relationship. This may be difficult, as it may evoke some painful or hard feelings directed toward yourself or your loved one. You may feel like you didn't do all you could have done for your loved one, for instance. Perhaps you feel like your loved one didn't do all she or he could for you. Either way, these feelings are quite likely to be difficult to approach or think about—and some of these things may raise feelings of guilt or remorse. Nevertheless, finding the courage and honesty to name and give voice to difficult feelings is an important step on the journey to emotional healing.

In the previous journal entry, you began to think about things connected to your relationship that are bothering you but which you can never go back and address in the way you might if your loved one were still alive. Those things are your unfinished business. Although thinking and writing about these things is a far cry from discussing and actually overcoming issues with your loved one, it is one route you do have available to you for getting the stuff *inside* of you *outside*. Once it is outside, you can begin to deal with it and perhaps take the sting away.

EXPRESSING YOUR FEELINGS

1. Complete the sentence for each feeling that applies to you. Add other feelings you may be having and an explanation. *I feel . . .*

angry because . . . _____

apologetic because . . . _____

ashamed because . . . _____

betrayed because . . . _____

cheated because . . . _____

crushed because . . . _____

curious because . . . _____

doubtful because . . . _____

exploited because . . . _____

guilty because . . . _____

hurt because . . . _____

irritated because . . . _____

mistreated because . . . _____

offended because . . . _____

regretful because . . . _____

resentful because . . . _____

vengeful because . . . _____

_____ *because . . .* _____

_____ *because . . .* _____

_____ *because . . .* _____

_____ *because . . .* _____

2. Take any one of these feelings or issues to elaborate on. Which of these issues is most pressing for you right now?

_____

_____

3. What makes this unfinished business for you?

_____

_____

_____

_____

_____

_____

4. What about this issue is left undone?

_____

_____

_____

_____

_____

_____

5. What do you want to say to your loved one about this piece of unfinished business?

_____

_____

_____

_____

_____

_____

THINGS TO THINK ABOUT

- Does thinking and writing about this issue help you better understand this piece of unfinished business?
- As you work on expressing your feelings, what other feelings are evoked for you? Do you feel guilty about your feelings, or do you feel a sense of relief?
- Does writing about this piece of unfinished business help get it off your mind? Do you need to revisit this piece of unfinished business again so that you can work on resolving your feelings about it?

Expressing Regret

Addressing unfinished business doesn't necessarily require endless hours of soul-searching to resolve complex emotional issues. Sometimes it requires no more than voicing regret for things done or things left undone.

You might think that naming things that you wish could change is an exercise in wishful thinking and futility, but this is not the case. Expressing regret isn't intended as a way to dwell on and wish away that which has passed. Instead, quite simply, it's a way to express sorrow—and sometimes remorse—for missed opportunity. It is a way to exorcize and relieve yourself of

> *Expressing regret isn't intended as a way to dwell on and wish away that which has passed. Instead, it's a way to express sorrow—and sometimes remorse—for missed opportunity.*

an otherwise unspoken burden. Expressing regret about things done or undone isn't the same as changing those things. The idea of dealing with unresolved feelings and unsettled issues isn't about changing what *was*, but rather it's about changing what *is*—helping you to alleviate the sometimes tremendous burden of unspoken regrets. The power of words rests in their ability to transform shapeless feelings into meaningful ideas and to bring them out into the world where they can be clearly seen.

REGRETS

I wish I'd said . . . _____

_____

I wish you'd said . . . _____

_____

I wish I had . . . _____

_____

I wish I hadn't . . . _____

_____

I wish you had . . . _____

_____

I wish you hadn't . . . _____

_____

I wish I could change . . . _____

_____

I'm sorry for . . . _____

_____

I wish . . . _____

_____

I wish . . . _____

_____

I wish . . . _____

_____

THINGS TO THINK ABOUT

- Are there things you can do about any of your unresolved regrets? Are there physical actions you can take in your life that might help you feel better about some of your regrets?
- Are there other problem situations in your life right now and current relationships—things unsaid or undone—that you need to be aware of and correct before they later become unresolved regrets?

Seeking Closure

As you move into the final stage of your grief work, you'll still be carrying many unresolved issues with you. You don't have to re-solve every issue and put all feelings behind you. But your ability to accept your loss, and the many unresolved issues and feelings that go with it, is key to your ability to move on with your life. Reclaiming and renewing your life requires that you put behind you the "baggage" of *this* relationship so that you may more fully experience and appreciate the other relationships in your life, old and new.

Your ability to accept your loss, and the many unresolved issues and feelings that go with it, is key to your ability to move on with your life.

If you find yourself stuck in this middle stage of grief, unable to accept or resolve old issues, it will be difficult—probably im-possible—to successfully tackle the tasks that lie ahead in your grief work—those of reclamation and reconciliation. If you're unable to get beyond your unfinished business and say good-bye, it may be time to turn back to your support network and get some help from others.

UNFINISHED BUSINESS

1. Are you ready to put closure on unfinished business with your loved one, or do you still have business to finish?

_____

_____

_____

_____

_____

2. Has this work left you feeling unsettled?

_____

_____

_____

_____

3. Do you need to forgive your loved one? Do you need to forgive yourself?

_____

_____

_____

_____

4. What will it take to finish unfinished business with your loved one?

_____

_____

_____

_____

5. Are you able to move on with your life? Are you ready to work toward reclamation and renewal, or do you feel you have more work to do with the tasks of this middle stage in your grief work?

_____

_____

_____

_____

_____

_____

_____

_____

THINGS TO THINK ABOUT

- Do you have unfinished business with the living?
- Are there journal entries in this chapter that you should be repeating?
- Is it too difficult to resolve unfinished business on your own? Do you need to turn to anyone for help?

Checking in with Your Road Map: Stage 3

As you work on the issues in this and other chapters, you're nearing the end of your work in Stage 2. As you approach the third and final stage of grief—reclamation and reconciliation—your tasks increasingly involve letting go, moving on, and renewing your life.

It's difficult to pinpoint exactly when Stage 3 begins. However, if you've worked through *The Healing Journey Through Grief* chapter by chapter, you're probably now at the point where you're resolving Stage 2 issues and starting to address the types of issues and tasks associated with Stage 3. The beginning of Stage 3 is generally marked by a reconnection, as you begin to engage more meaningfully with the people, things, and tasks that make up your daily life. You are now moving forward, renewing current relationships and building new ones. As you near the end of this stage, and your grief work in general, you'll experience "decathexis," as you pass a point at which your feelings no longer carry the intensity and weight they formerly did.

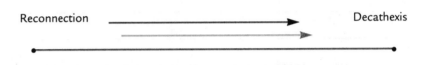

Stage 3: Reclamation and Reconciliation

The clearest indicator of successful grief work, and the "end" of this last stage, is your ability to live with the memory of your loss without it filling your thoughts and affecting your daily feelings and behaviors.

Regardless of when Stage 3 actually begins, you should understand that this final stage has no definitive end point: many aspects of your grief and loss will be absorbed into your life and carried with you always. You'll remember and carry with you the sadness of your loss, but the feelings will become memories and cease to burden you with the crushing and overpowering weight they once did.

The clearest indicator of successful grief work, and the "end" of this last stage, is your ability to live with the memory of your loss without it filling your thoughts and affecting your daily feelings and behaviors. Being able to move on and experience a meaningful life will signal the end of your grief work. When that time comes, it may cause a strange sensation. You may even feel some guilt as you realize that you're feeling better, but you'll be able to put even this in perspective and realize that this too is a "normal" part of the grief process and your recovery. Where are you now in your grief work?

CHECKPOINT: STAGES

She was no longer wrestling with the grief, but could sit down with it as a lasting companion and make it a sharer in her thoughts."—GEORGE ELIOT

Circle the letter that most closely describes where you are *right now* with each task.

Stage 1 Tasks	I'm not ready to deal with this task.	I'm working on this task.	I've completed this task.
Adjusting	A	B	C
Functioning	A	B	C
Keeping in check	A	B	C
Accepting support	A	B	C
Stage 2 Tasks			
Contending with reality	A	B	C
Development of insight	A	B	C
Reconstructing personal values and beliefs	A	B	C
Acceptance and letting go	A	B	C
Stage 3 Tasks			
Development of social relations	A	B	C
Decisions about changes in lifestyle	A	B	C
Renewal of self-awareness	A	B	C
Acceptance of responsibility	A	B	C

THINGS TO THINK ABOUT

- Where are you now with respect to Stage 2 and Stage 3 tasks? Are you more involved with tasks that deal with understanding and meaning or those concerned with the practical matters of rebuilding a life without your loved one? Are you somewhere between the stages or working on tasks that fall into both stages?
- Do you need to stay with the work of Stage 2 before moving on and dealing with Stage 3 tasks? Are you having any special difficulties with the issues and feelings of Stage 2?

14

Destination:

SEEING WITH NEW EYES

ISABELLE

John's death was awful enough, but in the chaos and confusion that followed I felt like I was drowning. The kids, his parents, the burial arrangements and funeral services, and all the life changes. On top of this terrible thing, I felt like there was all this noise, and all these people and things that needed attention. I had no time to think about what had happened to me.

I felt like I was on this crowded moving sidewalk, just being pushed along without being able to stop, get off, and look around. About two months after John died, I was in a bookstore, and I picked up a small book of verses at the sales counter while I was on line for the cashier. I'm glad I did because I found something special in what I read.

I bought that little book and put aside five minutes to read it every day. I miss John terribly, and with three young kids my life is still hectic. I haven't been able to put things back together and there are plenty of times when I feel totally overwhelmed. But the few minutes I take every day to think about myself and how I feel helps to strengthen me for the day ahead.

MUCH OF YOUR work in *The Healing Journey Through Grief* has been centered around the feelings, thoughts, and practical matters that have followed your loss. But not all grief work is centered around such concrete issues. Some grief work is not solution driven at all. Its focal point is on neither those feelings that are related to your loss nor the difficulties you may have faced since your loss. Instead, this part of your journey is simply about exploring your world, and through your environment finding ways to slow down, soothe, and rebuild your inner world. Journal entries in this chapter strengthen your ability to restore inner peace and find healing through quiet contemplation. They allow you to explore your place in the world around you, which is especially important at a time in your life when you may be struggling to find meaning, and perhaps feeling alone in that world without your loved one. These are exercises in self-reflection and self-restoration that will be useful long after your grief has fully resolved.

FIVE QUESTIONS

Think about five questions that you'd like answers to. They can be about life since your loss or about your loss itself. They can be about the meaning of the death or about how life might have been had your loved one not passed away. These five questions can be about anything relevant to your current life, for which you'd like answers.

Write each question here.

1. _____

2. _____

3. _____

4. _____

5. _____

Contemplation

"Know thyself" is a theme that's run throughout many cultures and systems of belief, dating back fourteen centuries in Western thought alone. It's a philosophy that has served as the basis for many personal enquiries, but there's a fine line between contemplation and rumination. The former involves reflection, a look inside, whereas rumination refers to a brooding inability to stop being introspective, or getting "stuck" inside.

What's the point of contemplation? It's a way to cease the activities of your everyday life, to look at and consider the things that surround you, to discover for yourself what works best for you, and to think about things that may have no answers. There are many ways to be contemplative. A quiet walk through a park, a day spent in an art museum exploring the unspoken messages of each painting, absorption in music, or closing your eyes to the outside world and reflecting on an internal thought or idea.

Not everyone is naturally contemplative, however. For some, slowing down and thinking in this way is just not part of their normal way of doing things. Nevertheless, there may be times when it's important to learn new ways of approaching and interacting with the world, to find ways to cope and manage that lie outside of the usual ways. A period of grief may be one of those times when the act and art of contemplation is what's needed to work through an extraordinarily difficult time.

Inspirational Words

What does it mean to be contemplative? To contemplate what, exactly? For many, the spoken or written words of others, captured as quotations, provide the basis for just such reflection. Often containing pearls of wisdom, quotations can help you understand how you're feeling, offer a new view of the world, help simplify confusing situations, and offer guidance and direction. In short, quotations are often inspirational, containing a simple wisdom in just a few words.

The quotations at the beginning of each chapter in *The Healing Journey Through Grief* and scattered throughout the book are used to illustrate the ideas in each chapter. In the following journal entry, pick three quotations that have particular meaning for you or move you in some way. There are many sources of quotations, from those used in this book to collected volumes that contain nothing but quotations. You can also find inspirational words in other places, such as stories or poems you've read, the lyrics of favorite songs, or the spoken words of people you know personally. Before you begin work on your next entry, think about some of your favorite passages, or search them out in preparation for the journal entry.

The entry that follows is one that you may want to repeat, using different quotations, so consider making copies of the blank entry before you use it.

WORDS OF WISDOM

1. Select three favorite or otherwise meaningful quotations and copy each here.

a. _____

_____

b. _____

_____

c. _____

_____

2. For this entry, pick one of these quotations to focus on: _____

3. What made you select this particular quotation for this entry?

_____

_____

4. How do these words have relevance to your life at this time?

_____

_____

_____

_____

_____

5. What do these words make you think of?

_____

_____

_____

_____

_____

6. In what ways can these words instruct you or offer you direction?

_____

_____

_____

_____

_____

THINGS TO THINK ABOUT

- Were you able to find three quotations that moved you? Was it easy or difficult to find sources for them?
- Were you able to understand why the quotation you chose for the entry affected you? Can this quote help you find direction or peace at this time in your life?
- Did you find meaning in the entry? Will you repeat it for the other two quotations you chose?

Daily Affirmations

Quotations sometimes provide the source for a "daily affirmation," one tool that many have learned to use for contemplation. An affirmation is an assertion of a truth, a belief, or an ideal—a way to put out an idea and commit yourself to it. Daily affirmations are usually based on a thought for that day, often inspirational or offering some form of guidance. They can provide a focal point for the entire day, to which you can return time and time again during the course of the day. Daily affirmations can be:

- energizing—helping you find the strength to work through difficult days

- inspirational—offering guidance and wisdom to help deal with daily issues

- self-affirming—reconfirming and strengthening your belief in yourself

- soothing—providing calming and comforting thoughts to focus on throughout the day

Morning affirmations set the pace for the day and provide an anchor to help you get through difficult times. Evening affirmations are a way to look back at, reflect on, and resolve the issues of the day. Between them, they're a powerful tool for finding and building emotional peace in your daily life.

Affirmations . . . are a powerful tool for finding and building emotional peace in your daily life.

Like your previous entry, the next journal entry requires some legwork before you can begin. This entry is to be completed daily, over a seven-day period. For the entry, collect seven inspirational verses that will serve as daily affirmations for each of the seven days. There are many sources for the affirmations including quotations, words from songs, poetry verses, scriptures, sayings, or other inspirational words. You can also refer to the books of verses and daily affirmations carried in many libraries and most bookstores. To complete the entry, you'll need to have your affirmation ready in advance of the day you use it, as you will refer back to it throughout each of the days.

DAILY AFFIRMATIONS

This is an entry to be completed over a seven-day period.

1. Each morning, write down your affirmation for that day. Write a few words that reflect on its meaning for you and the reason you chose these words as your affirmation for the day.

2. As you move through your day, think about how your day is going and how you're feeling. Each time you contemplate your day, recall your daily affirmation. Think about its meaning and why you chose it for that day.

3. At the end of your day, look back in contemplation. Think about the affirmation you chose. Was it helpful?

DAY 1

MY DAILY AFFIRMATION	WHY I CHOSE THESE WORDS
_____	_____
_____	_____
_____	_____
_____	_____
_____	_____

Importance of my daily affirmation (to be written at the end of the day):

_____

_____

_____

_____

DAY 2

MY DAILY AFFIRMATION	WHY I CHOSE THESE WORDS
_____	_____
_____	_____
_____	_____
_____	_____

Importance of my daily affirmation (to be written at the end of the day):

_____

_____

_____

_____

DAY 3

MY DAILY AFFIRMATION	WHY I CHOSE THESE WORDS
_____	_____
_____	_____
_____	_____
_____	_____

Importance of my daily affirmation (to be written at the end of the day):

_____

_____

_____

_____

DAY 4

MY DAILY AFFIRMATION	WHY I CHOSE THESE WORDS
_____	_____
_____	_____
_____	_____
_____	_____
_____	_____

Importance of my daily affirmation (to be written at the end of the day):

_____

_____

_____

_____

DAY 5

MY DAILY AFFIRMATION	WHY I CHOSE THESE WORDS
_____	_____
_____	_____
_____	_____
_____	_____

Importance of my daily affirmation (to be written at the end of the day):

_____

_____

_____

_____

DAY 6

MY DAILY AFFIRMATION

WHY I CHOSE THESE WORDS

_____

_____

_____

_____

Importance of my daily affirmation (to be written at the end of the day):

_____

_____

_____

_____

DAY 7

MY DAILY AFFIRMATION

WHY I CHOSE THESE WORDS

_____

_____

_____

_____

Importance of my daily affirmation (to be written at the end of the day):

_____

_____

_____

4. Did using daily affirmations help the contemplative process throughout and at the end of each day?

_____

_____

_____

_____

_____

THINGS TO THINK ABOUT

- Did you find it useful to use daily affirmations? Are you likely to continue using daily affirmations? If so, will you use them routinely or only during difficult times in your life?
- What did you learn about yourself through your week of daily contemplation? Did your daily affirmation help in the learning process?

Walking with Nature

At a time in your life when things are no longer normal, it's important to open yourself up to a side of life that you may not have noticed before. Finding meaning frequently requires looking at the same old things with different eyes. If you learn to do this, you may see all sorts of things in your life that you never noticed before. Learning to contemplate means learning to stop and examine. From contemplation can come action and growth.

A brisk walk is great exercise, but a *contemplative* walk exercises more than just your body—it exercises your senses and your mind as well. If you look, listen, and think, you'll notice all sorts of things that you might not have seen before. At this time in your life, a good walk may be just the thing you need—a way to open your senses and tune you in to those ordinary things

A brisk walk is great exercise, but a contemplative walk exercises more than just your body—it exercises your senses and your mind as well.

around you that can provide pleasure, comfort, and meaning. If you can apply these skills on a walk through nature, you can learn to use them in your everyday life too. A walk through nature, then, is another way of talking about a walk through your life.

The next journal entry takes you on a solitary walk through nature. Where you go will be up to you, but it should be a spot away from the paved streets, buildings, noises, and people of the community. Your walk could be along a trail in the woods, through the park, by a river, or in any quiet and relatively natural spot where you can be alone with yourself and your environment.

Plan to spend at least thirty minutes on your walk. Take a notebook and a pen with you. Read the questions asked by the next journal entry *before* you leave for your walk, and perhaps jot them down in your notebook. Be prepared to write the entire time you're on your walk. Every time you're struck by some smell, sight, or by a particular sound or thought, write it down. When your walk is over, complete the journal entry below.

A WALK ON THE QUIET SIDE

1. Describe your walk. Where did you go?

_____

_____

_____

_____

2. Describe the weather.

_____

_____

_____

_____

3. Describe the *feel* of the weather—the *mood* of the day.

_____

_____

_____

_____

4. On your walk, notice at least two colors that stand out for you. Describe them as you would to someone who can only see the world in black and white.

_____

_____

_____

_____

_____

5. What is it about these colors that is striking to you?

_____

_____

_____

_____

_____

6. As you walk, listen to the sounds your feet make as you walk. Listen for the sounds of insects and birds, the rustling of the breeze in the trees, or animals as they move through the woods. Listen for distant noises. Stop at least twice, and write down what you hear.

_____

_____

_____

_____

_____

7. Touch at least two things, and close your eyes. How do these things feel? What do they remind you of? Describe them to someone who has no sight.

_____

_____

_____

8. Smell the air. What odors are carried? Are they familiar smells? What do they make you think of?

_____

_____

_____

9. Look around you. Describe the sky. Is it one color, or does it change in hue as your eyes move from the horizon to overhead. Are there clouds? What's the *feel* of the sky?

_____

_____

_____

_____

10. Think about the contrast between the natural environment—those things that were there long before people came along—and the evidence of civilization—stone walls, telephone lines, the sounds of airplanes in the distance. How do they fit together?

_____

_____

_____

_____

11. Were there any special thoughts, questions, or answers that came up for you during your walk?

_____

_____

_____

_____

_____

_____

12. Describe your overall experience on this walk.

_____

_____

_____

_____

_____

13. What did you see that you'd never seen before?

_____

_____

_____

_____

14. What did you think about that you'd never thought about before?

_____

_____

_____

_____

- Will you take another contemplative walk through nature? Will you make walks like this part of your regular routine?
- Can you take a similar walk through your community—noticing things in your neighborhood that you've never before noticed or paid attention to?
- Did your walk through nature open your mind? What have you learned from this experience?

Talking to Yourself

The work in this chapter is intended to help you stop and think—about yourself, your life, your loss, and this time in your life. One way to do this is to find some time every day to think about what's going on around you in addition to what is going on inside you.

This next journal entry provides for a "running commentary" —an internal conversation. It begins with a single thought or question and keeps you connected to that original idea through-out the day. It's similar in some ways to a daily affirmation, but the goal here is not to find an inspirational thought to help you through the day but rather to find a way to stay in touch with your ideas and thoughts each day and to become more tuned in to yourself and your environment.

Purchase a small notebook that you can easily keep with you during the day. Write a question or thought on the first page of the notebook, and carry the pad with you throughout the day. Reread your question or thought at least five times during the day or whenever the original or related question or thought comes into your mind. Each time you reread the original question or thought, do one or more of the following.

- Write down an answer to your original question or a reply to your thought.

- Write down your additional thoughts on the subject.

- Write down a new, but related, question.

- Write down an answer, reply, or response to any new questions or thoughts you may have jotted down as the day progresses.

At the end of the day, review your original question or thought and all your subsequent work in your notebook. Spend a few minutes summarizing the work you completed for the day in this journal entry. Add a final reflective note to the day.

This journal entry provides a format that you can use repeatedly if you find that you like the entry and find it useful. You can use it as a daily diary or only on those days or during those times in your life when you need to find balance. Photocopy the blank format so that you can use it again.

A RUNNING COMMENTARY

1. Your original question or thought:

_____

2. Summarize how this day's running commentary developed.

_____

_____

_____

_____

_____

3. What have you learned from this day?

_____

_____

_____

_____

4. Describe an interesting observation you made on this day.

_____

_____

_____

_____

_____

THINGS TO THINK ABOUT

- Did your running commentary help you to stay in touch with your ideas, thoughts, or feelings throughout the day?
- Is there a thought you want to pursue as a running commentary for tomorrow?

Moving On

"My Sorrow, when she's here with me, Thinks these dark days of autumn rain Are beautiful as days can be; She loves the bare, the withered tree; She walks the sodden pasture lane."

—ROBERT FROST

The theme in this chapter has been on focusing—the ability to attach yourself to a thought, feeling, or experience and to use it as a vehicle to allow contemplation. Part of this process is to find places in your world that allow you to escape long enough to be contemplative. Consider the following questions.

- Have you found favorite spots or quiet locations that are meditative for you?
- Are there soothing sounds that can help you to relax and think?
- Are there solitary activities that help you to be reflective?
- Is there dance, art, poetry, literature, or music that can carry you away?
- Are there special words or favorite verses that can provide a focal point for contemplation?

FIVE ANSWERS

Do you have answers to the five questions you posed at the beginning of the chapter? If you do, there's no need to write them here, as you've already answered them. Instead, provide answers to the five questions that follow.

1. If you found answers to your five questions, do your answers help you feel better?

_____

_____

_____

_____

2. How can you best find answers?

_____

_____

_____

_____

_____

3. Is it always important to have answers?

_____

_____

_____

_____

_____

4. Are there some questions that have no answers?

_____

_____

_____

_____

_____

5. What can you do to live meaningfully even when you can't find answers?

_____

_____

_____

_____

_____

_____

THINGS TO THINK ABOUT

- What can you do if you can't find answers?
- Is finding answers dependent on asking the "right" kind of questions? Are you asking the "right" questions?

15

Destination:
RELATIONSHIPS

"The dead sleep in their moonless night; my business is with the living."
—RALPH WALDO EMERSON

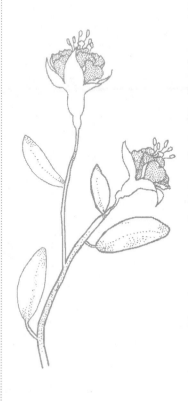

DONNA

I knew my father would eventually begin to see other women. He was less than sixty when my mother died, and I thought I wanted him to get involved with other people and start to date someday. But when I found out he was actually seeing someone else, it really threw me. It'd been over a year since mom died, and I wanted Dad to be happy. I mean, he was still relatively young, and we were all grown up with our own families. But I felt shocked, stung, and— I hate to admit it—angry when he told me he was seeing someone. I know this new relationship is important to him, but I don't know quite how to deal with it.

JACK

I kept thinking of this old song—"I'm feeling bad, because I'm feeling good." It's about a guy who starts to experience and enjoy life again but feels guilty because he thinks he should still be feeling rotten. When I first started feeling better, I was pleased and surprised. But after a while, I started wondering what it all meant. I got caught up in this kind of trap where I needed to move on, and was ready to, but then felt like I was abandoning my wife who died last year. When I actually met someone and got into a romance, I felt really guilty. Even though I was enjoying the relationship, I had a really tough time and several times decided to end that new relationship. I'm glad I didn't. What I really needed to do was handle my own guilt and accept that I was doing the right thing by moving on with the rest of my life.

ONE OF THE most significant aspects of life is social interaction—personal relationships that connect you to other people. In fact, without relationships it's hard to even think of someone as being a member of a society. In this chapter, the focus is on local relationships—ties with people at the community level.

As you move on with your life it's time to start thinking about, building upon, and perhaps renewing your current relationships and, more than likely, building new relationships as well.

Community is about shared values and experiences and an intimacy that exists among its members. You've already looked at some aspects of your community in terms of support and connection, but as you move on with your life it's time to start thinking about, building upon, and perhaps renewing your current relationships and, more than likely, building new relationships as well.

Reconfiguring Relationships

There are many relationships in your life, and there will be many more to come. In some respects, we define ourselves by our relationships. How you see yourself is quite likely affected deeply by your relationships—the more positive, gratifying, and supportive relationships you've had, the more likely you are to feel good about yourself. This isn't to say that good relationships are the be-all and end-all to positive self-image, but they're sure a powerful start. People who experience abusive relationships invariably don't feel good about themselves and often don't know how to handle or change their relationships or build new and positive ones.

Until now much of *The Healing Journey Through Grief* has focused on your relationship with the deceased. As you move on with your life, though, the focus needs to move to your relationships with others—those in your past, present, and future.

Even under the best of circumstances, it can be difficult to deal with relationships. And making sense of relationships is undoubtedly one of the most complex tasks you'll face in the final stage of your grief journey. You are going to face decisions about how to handle all sorts of relationships: those that are permanent; those that, without maintenance, may fade over time; and those new relationships that will come along and possibly supplant old ones. Each of these relationship variants comes loaded with emotional issues.

For instance, you may find your relationship with your loved one's family becoming increasingly distant over time, especially if they were not actively involved in your life to begin with. The same may be true for people who were primarily the friends of your loved one, rather than your own friends. These relationships may change because without your loved one, you may discover that you have little in common. Under different circumstances, these relationships may change because *you* don't want to maintain them. You may feel awkward being around these people now that your loved one is gone, or perhaps you don't like them and simply don't *want* a relationship.

It's also possible that you experience current or past relationships as holding you back from new ones or worry that you'll be judged by the "old" people for building new relationships. You may even feel guilty about new relationships. It could be very awkward, for example, to start dating someone new with your in-laws watching from the wings.

You may also find that others have come to depend on you in a way that is new; if you've been left a single parent, for instance, you may face substantial changes in the way you see yourself, the way others see you, and the sort of behavior that's now expected of you. Or perhaps the spouse of a deceased friend has come to depend on you for comfort, or an aging relative who's lost an adult child has turned to you for the support that was formerly given by the deceased.

Obviously, there are many possible scenarios that revolve around changed needs, expectations, and desires. But, whatever the specifics, it's quite common for old relationships to change over time —sometimes more quickly than others would expect. Part of your task is to understand how you feel about your relationships and how to ensure that your relationships are what you need them to be and, whenever possible, what you *want* them to be.

As you think about your current relationships, think about which ones are *important* and which are *satisfying*. Many people find that important relationships aren't always satisfying. A relationship with a parent or friend of your loved one, for instance, may be important in many respects but nevertheless fail to satisfy you on an emotional level. And, although relationships that satisfy usually *become* important relationships if they endure, sometimes they're short-lived or don't occupy an important place in your life. For instance, a work friendship may prove satisfying, but is nonetheless unimportant in your life as a whole. The ideal personal relationship is probably one that is both important *and* satisfying.

CURRENT RELATIONSHIPS

1. List five important relationships, and briefly describe why they're important.

Relationship   Important because . . .

a. _____   _____

_____

_____

_____

b. _____   _____
                                        _____
                                        _____
                                        _____
c. _____   _____
                                        _____
                                        _____
                                        _____
d. _____   _____
                                        _____
                                        _____
                                        _____
e. _____   _____
                                        _____
                                        _____
                                        _____

2. List current relationships that are satisfying, and briefly describe why.

Satisfying Relationship	*What Makes This Relationship Satisfying*

_____   _____

_____

_____

_____   _____

_____

_____

3. List current relationships that are dissatisfying, and briefly describe why.

Dissatisfying Relationship   *What Makes This Relationship Dissatisfying*

_____   _____

_____

_____

_____

_____   _____

_____

_____

_____

_____   _____

_____

_____

_____   _____

_____

4. In general, what do you seek from relationships? What makes a relationship satisfying to you?

_____

_____

_____

_____

_____

5. What is it about a relationship that eventually makes it dissatisfying for you?

_____

_____

_____

_____

6. What do you most want to change about any of your relationships in general?

_____

_____

_____

_____

_____

THINGS TO THINK ABOUT

- Are you generally satisfied by the relationships in your life at this time? If you're not, is it easy to be honest with yourself about relationships that dissatisfy?
- Are there some relationships in your life that may not satisfy you but are nevertheless important or permanent relationships? If so, is there anything you can do to improve the quality of them so that they meet more of your needs?

The Impact of Death on Relationships

Death is powerful. It can put distance between you and those in your community, and it can make you feel awkward and uncomfortable around others for whom the deceased was also a loved one. The circumstances of the death itself can raise issues within families that tear them apart, such as beliefs about the deceased or financial issues. The death of a loved one can also draw people closer, connecting them with others and making relationships more intimate than they were before the loss. It can solidify relationships, bind families, and unite communities. Death has the power to serve as either a symbolic beacon that pulls people together or a wedge that drives them apart.

Death has the power to serve as either a symbolic beacon that pulls people together or a wedge that drives them apart.

Of course, the power doesn't actually reside in the death itself. Rather, the power lies in the degree to which you allow your loss to affect your relationships and interactions. Although the consequences of the death are unavoidable, these relational effects—the emotional shaking up and loosening of ties—need not be permanent. As painful as it may be to acknowledge, in every tragedy lies the possibility of renewal (as in the story of the phoenix and its rebirth from the ashes). The effects of your loss on your community and relationships will ultimately be determined by you. However, building something out of the chaos that the death may have brought, and making the changes that you feel must be made, takes willingness and courage on your part.

Relationship Dynamics

It would be simplistic to think that changes in your relationships are brought about solely because of the death. Although your loss may be the catalyst, there are many other factors that affect relationships, both before and after the death. The word *dynamics* describes the way that people interact with each other—the "how" of interactions, usually hidden from sight.

The dynamics of a relationship are often unnoticed and unconscious; they rest in the interplay among the people in the relationship. The underlying current of a relationship can be built on positive factors—love, concern, compassion, and mutual attraction. But relational problems are often fueled by unspoken issues that might include jealousy, mistrust, unfulfilled desires, and insecurities. In any situation, one way to better understand relationships is to make visible the otherwise hidden dynamics. This goal requires that you understand and see those things about your relationships that normally lie hidden under the surface but nevertheless have an impact on (and even control) the way the relationship goes.

It would also be a mistake to think that understanding relationships is the same as having good relationships. If it was, every psychologist would have winning relationships that never failed. Nevertheless, whether you want to change or further develop an existing relationship, build a new relationship, or end a current one, understanding how relationships work—and how that *particular* relationship works—is an important tool.

As you explore your relationships, you'll be able to identify more easily what you need, what you want, and how you feel. It will also be essential for you to try to understand the point of view, feelings, and needs of the other person in the relationship. Relationships are a two-way street.

How has your loss affected your relationships? What other factors play into changing relationships and relationships you wish would change? In the next journal entry, you'll explore your relationships, the types of changes that have come about since your loss, and what you want from your relationships as you move into your life after the death.

This entry is one that will allow you to explore multiple relationships; accordingly, you may want to photocopy the blank format for repeated use.

As you explore your relationships, you'll be able to identify more easily what you need, what you want, and how you feel.

EVOLVING RELATIONSHIPS

1. My relationships have most changed because . . . _____

_____

_____

_____

_____

2. The way that my relationships have changed since the death is . . . _____

_____

_____

_____

_____

3. The relationships that have been affected the most are . . . _____

_____

_____

_____

_____

4. Some relationships may have been strengthened in some way since your loss, and others in some way weakened. Think about your relationships and why they've changed.

Strengthened Relationship	*Changed in What Way?*
_____	_____
_____	_____
_____	_____
_____	_____

Weakened Relationship	*Changed in What Way?*
_____	_____
_____	_____
_____	_____
_____	_____
_____	_____

5. Pick one of these relationships, and describe it further. You may repeat the entry for each relationship, if you choose. Relationship: _____

6. *This relationship has changed because . . .* _____

_____

_____

_____

7. *The impact of the death on this relationship has been . . .* _____

_____

_____

_____

8. *What I want most from this relationship is . . .* _____

_____

_____

_____

THINGS TO THINK ABOUT

- Do you have the power to bring about change in this relationship now? If so, how can you do this? *If not, what is impeding change?*
- Do you feel capable of overcoming the impact the death has had on your relationships?
- Should your focus be on restoring current relationships, building new ones, or both?

New and Changing Relationships

By now, you've been thinking about your relationships and how they may have changed, or are changing, since your loss. In some cases, you may be feeling *proactive*: you may actively want to renew old relationships, modify existing ones, or even end some altogether. As you move forward, you may be thinking about or be on the edge of pursuing one or more new relationships. On the other hand, relationships may be scary for you, and you may feel like you're constantly *reacting*, unable to get your needs met. You may feel as though you're on the "wrong" end of relationships—that you're not getting enough out of the ones you have, and aren't capable of forming new relationships. Or you may fear that the family and friends of your loved one are moving on without you, and you have less and less of a place in their lives.

These issues provide good examples of potentially difficult emotional situations. To deal effectively with relationships, you have to be open and honest with yourself, and this can be hard. You may have all sorts of feelings that are difficult to acknowledge. If you're insecure or unsure of yourself, for example, you may feel that you have no right to expect anything from anyone else, or you may wonder why anyone would want to have a more significant relationship with you. At the other extreme, if you're feeling dissatisfied with some of your relationships and want more from them, you may feel callous or that you've "used" people—especially if you're seeking more distance from or an end to relationships with people to whom you feel you owe something.

As you move on with your life, there's also the distinct possibility that you'll feel guilty as you seek out, respond to, and build new relationships. You may feel you're letting others down or leaving them behind, or you may feel that you're being judged by

Relationships may be scary for you, and you may feel like you're constantly reacting, *unable to get your needs met.*

others as you rebuild your life. You may even feel as though you're somehow betraying others, including your loved one. These are hard-to-deal-with issues. The role of your journal here is to help you put your thoughts onto paper where you can see them and figure out for yourself what you want, how to best pursue it, and when. Your journal is your private place to pursue and explore these matters. It's imperative that you write openly and honestly *now* and deal with your insecurities and guilt *later.* Hiding thoughts and feelings from yourself won't help you deal with them.

The next two entries provide you with a format for exploring your relationships further and perhaps making decisions about them. Because they allow you to deal with multiple relationships, again you may want to copy the blank formats for repeated use.

REMAKING RELATIONSHIPS

Think about the relationships you've explored in previous journal entries. Select an existing relationship that you want to change in some way.

1. Relationship with: _____

2. What sort of change are you looking for?

_____ improvement   _____ change the relationship in some way

_____ gain distance from the relationship   _____ end the relationship

other: _____

3. What's motivating your desire to change this relationship?

_____

_____

_____

_____

4. Describe the change you want in more detail.

_____

_____

_____

5. In what ways does this relationship not meet your present needs?

_____

_____

_____

6. What do you think the other person wants or needs from this relationship?

_____

_____

_____

7. How will changes affect the other person?

_____

_____

_____

8. If this is a relationship that _can't_ be changed, what can you do to improve the situation for yourself?

_____

_____

_____

_____

9. What sorts of things stand in the way of making the changes you want?

_____

_____

_____

_____

_____

_____

_____

THINGS TO THINK ABOUT

- It can be emotionally difficult to explore relationship issues. Have you been honest with yourself as you've been working on these entries? How have you dealt with any difficult emotions that may have come up?
- Do you feel like you have to make changes of any kind in your relationships? If so, how will you tackle these? Do you have anyone you can talk to about some of these changes?

New Relationships

It's inevitable that new relationships will come into your life. In many cases, you'll enter these with ease. But under other circumstances, new relationships may be difficult to deal with. If your romantic partner has died, for example, a new romantic relationship may well lead to internally conflicting feelings. Similarly, if you find yourself making new friends, you may feel guilt because you're leaving old ones behind. If you're a bereaved parent, you may experience especially difficult feelings as you face the prospect of giving birth again or adopting a child. But the issue is not whether you *should* enter into new relationships; rather, it is *when, how,* and *with whom*.

MOVING ON

1. Are you ready for new relationships?

_____

_____

_____

_____

2. What new relationships do you want to build?

_____

_____

_____

_____

3. Why are you seeking a new relationship? What's the motivation?

_____

_____

_____

_____

4. Do you feel conflicted about the possibility of a new relationship?

_____

_____

_____

_____

5. Describe your feelings about seeking or having a new relationship.

_____

_____

_____

_____

6. What are your hopes for new relationships?

_____

_____

_____

_____

7. What's stopping you from seeking or getting involved in a new relationship?

_____

_____

_____

_____

8. What are your fears about a new relationship?

_____

_____

_____

_____

9. Is there a new relationship in particular that comes to mind? If so, write a little about that relationship now.

_____

_____

_____

_____

_____

_____

_____

_____

- There are many kinds of relationships. When you think about new relationships, what comes to mind?
- Are others in your circle ready for you to build new relationships? How will you deal with resistance or family members who may judge you or disapprove of new relationships?

The Relationships of Others

In this chapter, you've dealt with changes in *your* relationships, and the development of new relationships in your life. In many cases, however, you're part of a community of other people who are also experiencing a sense of loss through this death. As you move on with your life, you'll discover that others in your circle are moving on with theirs also. This can lead to emotional and relational difficulties.

In some cases, you may be on the "receiving" end of the changes that one or more of those people may be making. There may be less room for you in *their* lives, or they may be forming new relationships of their own. For example, many children—teenage and adult children alike—experience difficulties when they learn that their widowed parent is beginning to date again.

As you complete your work in this chapter, think about how well you're dealing with the relationship changes that others in your circle may be making. Is your emotional well-being connected to these relationships? How can you deal with *their* changes?

CHECKPOINT: RELATIONSHIPS

1. What issues are you experiencing with the way you're being treated by others who are sharing your loss?

_____

_____

_____

_____

2. If it applies, how well are you dealing with new relationships that others in your life may be making?

_____

_____

_____

_____

3. Is it important for you to talk directly to other people in your circle about your relationships or theirs?

_____

_____

_____

_____

4. As you complete this chapter, how are you feeling about your relationships or the relationships of others?

_____

_____

_____

_____

5. Are there unaddressed relationship issues still hanging for you?

_____

_____

_____

_____

_____

_____

THINGS TO THINK ABOUT

- New situations often accompany new relationships. Have you thought about new situations in your life? Are you ready for such changes?
- If you're having difficulties knowing what to do or how to deal with changing or new relationships, can you talk to someone? Who? How much will you share?

16

Destination:
MOVING ON

"Sadness flies on the wings of the morning and out of the heart of darkness comes the light."
—JEAN GIRAUDOUX

DANNY

Sandy died after a pretty debilitating illness. It took so much out of her, and it took a lot out of the rest of us too. She was the center of our family life—a great mom, a great wife to me, and a wonderful friend. She was active in the community, and she was really close to her parents and brothers.

It was really difficult for me to make the decision for us to move on, but after a while I knew I had to set myself and my family on a new course, and that we all deserved another chance to live our lives fully. Of all people, Sandy wouldn't have wanted her memory to hold us back. The day I made the decision to sell the house, give up the business, and move across country was probably the toughest day I'd faced since Sandy's death. But the house was empty without her, and so were our lives. As a family, we decided that it was time to build our life without Sandy.

It was really one hard decision after another—including moving away from Sandy's parents and family—but the time had come. That was three years ago. The guilt has passed now, the kids are older and moving into their adulthood and further into their

235

own lives, and I look back with pride on our ability to accept our loss and move on with our lives.

YOU'RE AT A time in your life now where you've probably fallen back into a daily routine of some kind, and most people expect you to be pretty much over your grief. It's not that anyone expects you not to still have strong feelings about your loss, but you're certainly expected to have been able to return to some version of your life before the death. In other words, although you're not "over" your loss—and may never be—you are able to function much as anyone else.

This is a reasonable expectation. If grief is still actively interfering with your daily life, then you probably shouldn't be attempting to work in this chapter. By now, your grief work should have taken you through many of the steps required to be able to function once again, and you should be prepared to think about the *rest* of your life rather than those parts that have passed.

Decisions and Choices

Every death brings a different set of circumstances. The circumstances of your life since your loss will define the sort of life choices that are open to you now—decisions you *must* make and decisions you *can* make. What's the difference?

Decisions that must be made include those compulsory decisions that are inescapable. If you've been left a single parent, for example, you'll have to make decisions about what to do next. Life requires it. But you almost certainly will have choices about the kinds of decisions to make. For instance, if your aging parent has been widowed, your decision choices might include having your parent live with you or another relative, hiring a home health aide, purchasing a home for your parent in a senior living community, or placing your parent in a nursing home.

The circumstances of your life since your loss will define the sort of life choices that are open to you now—decisions you must *make and decisions you* can *make.*

In other circumstances, you have the *option* of making choices. These are choices that reflect lifestyle decisions, and they are not mandatory. Moving to another community or switching jobs are examples of these intentional decisions. You don't have to make these decisions, but they're often personally appealing or enhance the way you choose to live.

Whether they are compulsory or optional, decisions mean making choices. There's no way to advise you as to the "correct" decision to make or the "right" course to take. In fact, there's often more than one "correct" decision and more than one "wrong" choice. But there are certainly guides to decision making that can help you to think about and arrive at an *appropriate* decision for you.

- Recognize that you have choices in the first place. Most of the time, you're not simply a recipient of the way things "have" to be.

- Consider the nature of the problem that you're trying to resolve. Every decision is a *response* to a particular situation: what is the issue, problem, or situation you need to address?

- Think of all the possible choices you have. In brainstorming, the goal is simply to list every possible choice, including the outlandish ones. In this step, your job is to be creative—what decisions *could* be made?

- List the rational and realistic choices. Break your list of possible decisions into those that are really unrealistic at this time and those that are within the realm of possibility.

- Evaluate your choices. Now think about the possible decisions that you can realistically make. Which most fit the particular circumstances of the problem you're trying to resolve, and which best fit your present life? If only one choice comes up, your decision may be clear.

- Consider the consequences. What are the downsides to your possible decision choices? Who will be affected by your choice, and how? How will your possible choices affect your life, your finances, your relationships, and so on?

- Reflect on the decision you're planning to make. What will it feel like to actually take those steps and make that choice? What will it feel like not to make that choice? Is the decision you're pondering permanent, or is it reversible?

The next set of things to think about will lead you to an "action plan." They will help you discover how actually to implement your decision.

- Consider the obstacles. What barriers will you face in making this choice, and what obstacles will you have to overcome?

- Outline your implementation plan. What steps will you have to undertake to actually make your choice happen? What will you have to do to implement your choice?

DECISIONS, DECISIONS, DECISIONS

1. Think about *current* decisions and choices in your life. What types of decisions are the hardest to make?

_____

_____

_____

_____

2. In what way has the death of your loved one led to the choices you're currently facing?

_____

_____

_____

_____

3. In what ways has the death of your loved one opened up your life to the possibility of change?

_____

_____

_____

_____

_____

4. What opportunities for change are in your life right now?

_____

_____

_____

_____

_____

5. What changes would you generally like to make?

_____

_____

_____

_____

_____

6. In general, what things in your current life force you, or limit your ability, to make decisions?

_____

_____

_____

_____

_____

7. What stops you from making changes?

_____

_____

_____

THINGS TO THINK ABOUT

- Are the life decisions that you face now the result of your loss, or are they typical of the kinds of decisions you faced before the death?
- Are the difficulties you currently face in making choices connected to your loss, or are they typical of decision-making difficulties you faced even before the death?
- Are the *circumstances* of your life now inhibiting your ability to make change, or do you need to change your general *approach* to decision making?

The Impact of Your Decisions

As you think about decisions and your choices, consider three factors: responsibility, spontaneity, and consequences.

In some ways, making decisions about your life can be summed up quite simply: now that your life has changed, where do you want to be, what do you want to be doing, and who do you want to be doing it with? As you go through the process of remaking your life and moving on, you'll find your journal can be a useful tool for laying out, exploring, and generally considering your options. As you think about decisions and your choices, consider three factors: responsibility, spontaneity, and consequences.

RESPONSIBILITY

Compulsory decisions—the "must" decisions—have already been described as inescapable. But, of course, nothing is inescapable, except death itself. Everything is avoidable to those who want to deny their responsibilities. The "must" decisions are intimately connected to the acceptance of personal responsibility.

If death has left a situation in your life that must be addressed, you can, of course, choose to pretend it doesn't exist. It's no surprise to hear that people don't always take care of their responsibilities and often actively try to avoid them. Nevertheless, this doesn't alter the reality of their situations, and it usually means that they—or someone else—will suffer as a result of their lack of responsible action. When you make decisions, especially consider who will be affected and for whom you may be responsible.

SPONTANEITY VERSUS IMPETUOUSNESS

Sometimes there's no reason in the world not to act on a whim or make a quick choice. It's healthy to be spontaneous at times, and some situations simply call for a sudden, spur-of-the-moment decision. On the other hand, acting without thinking can be impetuous, particularly if the consequences are given little consideration or none at all.

Both spontaneous and impetuous behaviors can have positive, negative, or neutral effects, and it can be argued that there's little difference between the two words. But the difference lies in the intent. Whereas spontaneity is generally thought of as harmless and even refreshing, we usually think of impetuous behavior as thoughtless and potentially problematic.

As you make decisions, think about the difference between the two words. Decisions that affect your life and the lives of others should be carefully considered. It's often a poor idea to make decisions when you're under a great deal of pressure or following sudden life changes. On the other hand, don't delay deciding indefinitely or you'll risk getting "stuck." Try to pick a time and place in the feasible future to make the decision, and then make it.

LONG-TERM EFFECTS

Finally, take into account that decisions you make now may have effects that stay with you a long time. Buying a new wardrobe of clothes, seeking a new career, or moving from one home to another in the same community may involve some deep decision making, but none represents necessarily radical changes. Selling your home and moving to another state, divorcing your spouse, or giving up your job are far more significant decisions in terms of their long-term impact and are often difficult to reverse later.

The next journal entry is intended to help you think about individual decision choices, as well as your decision-making style in general. Copy the blank format if you think you may want to repeat the entry to think through the same decision choice from more than one perspective or to consider other decisions.

MAKING DECISIONS

1. Briefly describe one situation or problem that you're currently trying to resolve.

_____

_____

_____

_____

2. What choices do you have to resolve this issue? Name eight different decision choices.

a. _____   e. _____

b. _____   f. _____

c. _____   g. _____

d. _____   h. _____

3. Review the choices you've just identified, and select the four most rational and realistic choices. Under each, describe how this choice could fit the circumstances and reality of your life.

a. _____

This solution fits because . . . _____

_____

b. _____

This solution fits because . . . _____

_____

c. _____

This solution fits because . . . _____

_____

d. _____

This solution fits because . . . _____

_____

4. Now select just one of these choices, and use it as the focal point for the remainder of this entry.

_____

5. Think about the possible consequences of this choice. Is there a price to pay? If so, what is it?

_____

_____

_____

_____

_____

_____

6. If you made this choice, what challenges and obstacles will you have to overcome to make this decision work?

_____

_____

_____

_____

_____

7. If you make this choice, what will you have to do to make it a reality?

_____

_____

_____

_____

_____

8. How will your life be affected by this choice?

_____

_____

_____

_____

_____

9. Is there anyone else whose life will be affected by this decision? If so, who, why, and how?

_____

_____

_____

_____

_____

THINGS TO THINK ABOUT

- Has this entry helped you to better understand the issues and choices involved in this decision?
- What stops you from making a choice and acting on it in this case?
- Can you afford to take a chance on this decision, or are the consequences irreversible?
- Are you giving this decision too little thought (are you being impetuous) or too much thought (are you being indecisive)?

Telling the World

By now you've had the chance to think about and express your loss, to explore life after and since the death of your loved one, and to consider where you want or need to go now, and with the help of the previous entry, you should be able to make good choices for yourself and your future. But as you move further into your life, what's been left unsaid or undone? You may have written an obituary, and you may have found a suitable way to commemorate and memorialize your loss. Even so, as you near the end of this journal, it's important to provide a way to wrap up this part of your healing journey and put closure on it.

For all you've said and written already, what last words are there, and what final good-byes? What do you want to tell others about how you're feeling *now* with respect to what you've been through on your healing journey and how it's affected you?

IF ONLY YOU KNEW WHAT'S INSIDE OF ME NOW:
A LETTER TO THE WORLD

Day: _____ Date: _____

I want you to know that . . . _____

_____

_____

_____

_____

_____

_____

_____

_____

_____

If you knew what was inside of me now, you'd know . . . _____

_____

_____

_____

_____

_____

_____

_____

My grief journey has left me feeling . . . _____

_____

_____

_____

_____

_____

_____

_____

_____

_____

_____

THINGS TO THINK ABOUT

- Are there other ways you need to be public or share your experiences with others?
- Is there still more you need to say about your loss?
- Have you considered sharing some of your experiences, and sharing the stories that others have to tell, through a grief support group?

Saying Good-bye

In the end, closure means just that—putting a final face onto something, whether it be a time in your life, a place left behind, or a relationship. Closure means finding a way to feel complete as you move on and leave a part of your life behind.

Little in life is more final than saying good-bye. Here, though, you're not saying good-bye to your memories, your connection, or your ability to revisit your loved one many times over in many different ways. You're not even saying good-bye to your ability and right to keep talking to your loved one or your desire to keep your relationship alive and important in its own way.

What you are doing is saying good-bye to those parts of the relationship that have ended and can be revisited only in memory. Saying good-bye is a way of recognizing that there are some questions that can't be answered and some things that can't be said. The very act of saying good-bye is a way to finish unfinished business. In the next journal entry, write a farewell letter to your loved one. Although you can always write another letter at a later point, don't complete this entry until you're ready to say good-bye and let go.

Saying good-bye is a way of recognizing that there are some questions that can't be answered and some things that can't be said.

A GOOD-BYE LETTER

Date: _____

To: _____

I will always remember . . . _____

_____

_____

_____

_____

_____

Before you left, I wish . . . _____

_____

_____

_____

_____

Your death left me feeling . . . _____

_____

_____

_____

_____

I want you to know that . . . _____

_____

_____

_____

_____

Now finish your letter. Write it free form, and say anything you want to.

_____

_____

_____

_____

_____

_____

_____

_____

_____

_____

_____

THINGS TO THINK ABOUT

- Reread your letter. Does it feel satisfying? Did you say what you wanted to? Is there more you want to say? Will you write another letter?
- Are you ready to say good-bye? Do you want to return to this journal entry at a later time, and rewrite your letter?

17

As One Journey Ends, Another Begins

"Weeping may endure for a night, but joy cometh in the morning."
—PSALMS 30:5

THE END OF this journal marks the end of your grief work in general. As you reach this point, however, you've really only completed one step in a lifelong journey. What you've been through and what you've learned through your grief work sets the pace for the journey that lies ahead.

If your encounter with grief has left you emotionally intact, then you're in good shape for the things that are yet to come— that which doesn't harm you only makes you stronger. If your grief work has offered enlightenment, fostered personal growth, and even enriched your life, then all the better. For you, something has been born out of death and sorrow.

If your journey has left you emotionally shaky and uncertain, consider getting help. There are many sources of assistance, including grief support groups, individual counselors, clergy, and other professional caregivers. Grief support groups offer a cooperative, communal, and sensitive environment for sharing and interacting with others in similar situations. But this kind of help is not only for those who continue to feel the devitalizing impact of grief. Individual counseling, for example, provides many people

with a useful way to explore unresolved issues, uncertainties, and life decisions. All these helping environments offer a great deal for many people.

Where will your life take you now? If you've used your grief journal through this difficult time, then you've no doubt found it useful. It may have served many purposes—a place to express and explore feelings, a guide to help direct you through your grief and help share your decisions, a narrative of your life in troubling times, a mirror to reflect your relationships and inter-actions with others, a means of learning new ways to see your-self and the world around you. If you've come this far in *The Healing Journey Through Grief*, then you've found value in the journaling process. Will your journal continue to be a useful tool and valuable companion as you continue along your lifelong journey?

If your encounter with grief has left you emotionally intact, then you're in good shape for the things that are yet to come.

MY JOURNAL

1. How has your journal been most useful?

_____

_____

_____

_____

_____

2. Have certain types of journal entries been more useful than others?

_____

_____

_____

_____

3. What's been the most difficult aspect of journaling for you?

_____

_____

_____

_____

_____

4. What's been the most fulfilling aspect of journaling?

_____

_____

_____

_____

_____

5. Overall, describe your experience keeping this journal.

_____

_____

_____

_____

_____

6. *My journal . . .* _____

_____

_____

_____

_____

_____

_____

_____

"We shall not cease from exploration
And the end of all our exploring
Will be to arrive where we started
And know the place for the first time."

—T. S. ELIOT

As you put this part of your life behind you—not your loved one or the memories of your relationship, of course, but your *grief*—it's time to look ahead. What do you see? As you peer into the future, you may find that looking into the past helps.

What have you gained from the sad experience of loss? In what ways have you grown as an individual, and what have you learned from your grief?

I'VE LEARNED

From my grief, I've learned . . . _____

_____

_____

_____

_____

I'm not the same person as I was because . . . _____

_____

_____

_____

_____

My greatest lesson has been . . . _____

_____

_____

_____

_____

_____

About myself I've learned . . . _____

_____

_____

_____

_____

_____

About others I've learned . . . _____

_____

_____

_____

_____

_____

From my grief, I . . . _____

_____

_____

_____

_____

_____

_____

- Was this a difficult entry to complete? If it was, what made it difficult? Was it an important entry?
- Can you honestly say you've learned something from your loss? If you can, do you know what it is you've learned?
- Have you grown as a person because of your grief? In what ways?

"A deep distress hath humanized my soul."
—WILLIAM WORDSWORTH

In completing this book you've accomplished a great deal. You've taken significant steps down the path to healing, self-help, and personal growth. As your personal journey continues, the lessons and methods learned in this book will help you along the way.

Where will your healing journey take you next, and what tools or people will you need to help you along that path?

About the Author

PHIL RICH, EdD, MSW, holds a doctorate in applied behavioral and organizational studies and is a clinical social worker diplomate with a master's degree in social work. Over the past two decades, he has worked as a director of treatment programs, a clinical supervisor, and a practicing therapist. He is currently actively involved with inpatient care at the Brattleboro Retreat, and maintains a private outpatient practice in western Massachusetts.

Acknowledgments

THERE ARE ALWAYS many people to thank. But the single person who stands out the most, and the person to whom I am the most appreciative, is Kelly Franklin of John Wiley & Sons, without whom there would be no Healing Journey.

I also must thank my wife and great friend, Bev, who gave me much help with this book, and was patient with and supportive of me, as she always is. Thanks also to my lovely daughter, Kaye, who is always interested in my work, always curious, and ever willing to give up her time on our computer so I can work.

This particular book is dedicated in respectful memory of Ed, Ina, Marion, and Steve, and all those who survive them.